CW00404189

✱✱✱✱✱✱✱

WITH HIM ...

IN HIM

✱✱✱✱✱

Father Jonathan Eric Moore

"With Him….in Him"

…………...an old priest meanders through the Sunday Gospels

Year B (Saint Mark) Part 1

Advent 2023 to Pentecost 2024

Father Jonathan Eric Moore

Glossop, Derbyshire 2023

Dedication

To Father Francis Maple OFM Cap., without whose help and encouragement this book would never have been attempted.

Introduction

In the chapel of Saint Mary's College, Oscott on Trinity Sunday 1974 Archbishop George Patrick Dwyer conferred the Order of Deacon upon sixteen young men, among them one Jonathan Eric Moore. As deacons we were commissioned both to proclaim the Good News. I spent the summer of that year in the parish of Saint Joseph's Retford, under the tutelage of Father Daniel Clavin, a gentle man of deep spirituality. I used to write my homilies very carefully each week on a small portable typewriter – personal computers and word processors were still a long way into the future, and far beyond my means. The text of none of those early homilies has survived, which is probably just as well!

Fifty years on, I still write out a homily in full every week. I don't have the talent of being able to stand up without so much as a note and speak 'off the cuff", and don't suppose I ever will have now.

My first appointment as a priest in 1975 was with the late Monsignor Provost Humphrey Wilson, who had served as a Guards officer in the First World War. He always wrote out his homilies in full, and approved of my doing so too. He used to say "It's easy enough *starting* an impromptu homily, but a deuce of a job *finishing* it!". His great friend was Father Clifford Howell SJ, a man of wit and learning. It was a pleasure to hear him preach when he visited, and there may be echoes of him still in this little book.

Canon James Columba Cantwell, late of the Catholic Missionary Society, was my next Parish Priest. He too was a powerful and engaging preacher, who used to tell his Curates: "Prepare your words well beforehand, lads – a bird that's hatched on a Saturday night won't fly far the following morning!"

They have all gone to God now, but certainly influenced me. The discipline of homily writing has meant that I have quite a good supply to choose from now.

I have resisted any encouragement to compile a book of homilies up until now, but yielded to the requests of Father Francis Maple OFM Cap and several other friends this year. This is the first part of a collection of homilies for lectionary Year B, Saint Mark, and contains a homily for each Sunday between Advent 2023 and Pentecost 2024.

If God spares me, it is my hope to continue this work into 2025 and 2026 in thanksgiving to Him for so many long and joyful years in ministry.

Acknowledgements:

Old and New Testament, except where indicated are from the Catholic Public Domain Bible (2009). My personal thanks to Ronald L. Conte Jnr, who placed his modern translation of the edition of the Latin Vulgate Bible (Hertzenauer 1914) in the Public Domain and thus free of all restriction in usage. Furthermore, I am grateful for his permission to alter spelling where necessary to current English usage.

Psalms and Canticles from The Revised Grail Psalms, copyright 2010 Conception Abbey/The Grail. My thanks are due to Mary Sperry at the Catholic Bishops Conference of the USA for permission to do so.

I am also grateful to Hymns Ancient and Modern for permission to quote from Dr. William Barclay, The Gospel of John, Volume 1, copyright William Barclay 2009, published by St. Andrew Press.

As far as I am aware, all other quotations are in the public domain. If I am mistaken in any instance, I offer my unreserved apologies and will make good my error forthwith.

Jonathan Moore

Advent 2023

1st Sunday of Advent   *'Spiritual Stocktaking'*

Gospel Reading: Mark 13:33-37

Today's short Gospel might be seen as no more than a summary of those we have heard in recent weeks, urging us to be prepared, to stand ready to welcome the Master when He comes. It would, however, be a mistake to conclude that it tells us nothing new. Advent is the time of preparation, a time for self-examination. All around us we see the annual "dying" of nature, but we are called to renewed efforts in Christian living. Saint Teresa of Avila tells us very clearly that we cannot enter deeply into the spiritual life unless we have passed through what she calls "The Room of Self-Knowledge." (*The Interior Castle, First Mansions, Chapter 1 tr. Benedict Zimmerman, pub Thomas Baker, London 1921*). When the Greek philosopher Socrates was on trial for his life, he famously remarked "An unexamined life is not worth living" (Plato *Apologia* 35a5). We are accustomed to think, quite rightly, of Advent as a time for examination of one's conscience. True self-knowledge, however, demands that we go further than just totting up our sins: it is not simply about the things we do or fail to do, it is a matter of who we think we are in relation to God, and that calls for what I like to call "Spiritual Stocktaking".

There are three passages in our Mass readings today which help us to do this:

1. *And now, O Lord, you are our Father, yet truly, we are clay. And you are our Maker, and we are all the works of your hands. (Isaiah 64:8)*

It is vitally important to know ourselves as God's creation. We did not make ourselves; being born was not our choice, neither was the family unit and society in which we found ourselves. We had no choice in our gender, the colour of our skin, our eyes or our hair (though I believe some people later resort to dyes and bleaches!). Psychologists tell us that our character and personality were largely determined before we even started school, so they weren't a matter of choice either. We **are** who we **are**. Saint Paul tells the Romans: *"Will what is moulded say to its moulder 'Why have you made me like this?'"* (Romans 9:21). We neither made nor formed ourselves. There is a great temptation to deny who we are, or to try and "re-invent" ourselves. It is also very easy to fall into the trap of wasting our lives trying to cross-examine God (Why does this or that happen in the world? Why does God not cure my illness? Why are there terrible wars?). It is very important to be aware of the futility of such questioning. We often misunderstand the reason for our discontent with ourselves and our world. Nothing short of God Himself can truly satisfy us. "He made us, we belong to Him" (Psalm 100:3)

2. *By that grace, in all things, you have become wealthy in him, in every word and in all knowledge. (1 Corinthians 1:7)*

The philosopher Kierkegaard said: "I can only understand my life looking back, and yet I must live forwards.....my focus should be on what I do in life, not knowing everything, except what I do." (Journal, July 1835). In other words, we cannot hope to understand the meaning of our lives as we lead them. Answers will come later, but what God asks of us right now is to live by faith. Our life of faith and trust in God is only made possible by the gift of the Holy Spirit. In his letter to the Galatians (5:22), Saint Paul speaks of the Fruits of the Holy Spirit:

"But the fruit of the Spirit is charity, joy, peace, patience, kindness, goodness, forbearance, meekness, faith, modesty, abstinence, chastity."

Despite the unpredictability and disappointments of life, Christians can always call with confidence upon the Holy Spirit to give them the strength to live <u>as they are, where they are, in the way God wants.</u>

3. In the Gospel we just heard, Jesus told us that this time of waiting is like being the servants of a man who has left his servants... each with his own task.

There is a beautiful passage in Blessed John Henry Newman's "Meditations and Devotions" (*Hope in God, March 7, Longmans 1908*):

God has created me to do Him some definite service; He has committed some work to me which He has not committed to another. I have my mission—I never may know it in this life, but I shall be told it in the next. Somehow I am necessary for His purposes, as necessary in my place as an Archangel in his—if, indeed, I fail, He can raise another, as He could make the stones children of Abraham. Yet I have a part in this great work; I am a link in a chain, a bond of connexion between persons. He has not created me for naught. I shall do good, I shall do His work; I shall be an angel of peace, a preacher of truth in my own place, while not intending it, if I do but keep His commandments and serve Him in my calling.

Therefore I will trust Him. Whatever, wherever I am, I can never be thrown away. If I am in sickness, my sickness may serve Him; in perplexity, my perplexity may serve Him; if I am in sorrow, my sorrow may serve Him. My sickness, or perplexity, or sorrow may be necessary causes of some great end, which is quite beyond us. He does nothing in vain; He may prolong my life, He may shorten it; He knows what He is about. He may take away my friends, He may throw me among strangers, He may make me feel desolate, make my spirits sink, hide the future from me—still He knows what He is about.

Taken with our readings today, Cardinal Newman's words give us a wonderful theme for our own meditations this first week of Advent:

God made you - God doesn't make junk, you are *"His workmanship"* (Ephesians 2:10)

God knows you better than you know yourself.

God loves you just as you are.

God's grace helps you to grow in holiness

God knows what He is doing.

****

2nd Sunday of Advent. *Awaiting the Blessed Hope*

Gospel Reading Mark 1:1-8

Do you know the story of Pandora's Box? It is one of the Ancient Greek myths. Pandora was given a box to take care of but told she must never ever open it. Being a curious sort of lady, she decided to take a little peek, opened the lid, and released all of the miseries of the world, which flew out in a great cloud. When they had gone, Pandora found that only one thing remained in the box, and that was Hope.

Pope Francis has observed that it is not so much true to say "While there's life there's hope" as "Where there's hope there's life" (General Audience, May 31st 2017). The story of Pandora in only a myth, but the misery, disappointment and tragedy of human existence is only too real. Without hope, life is not worth living.

At times, our world can seem a place where hope cannot survive. There was surely never a time when worldly hope was scarcer - countries are divided, nuclear weapons and missiles increase, civil war annihilates whole communities and sends refugees fleeing, hungry children are ignored because their needs are of no interest to the powerful, human beings are trafficked by the thousands to be used for sex or cheap labour, and we are faced with the truth of the dreadful damage we are causing to our planet and environment -

surely we need hope more than ever!

Advent calls us to focus on the one hope which will never disappoint us, the presence of Our Lord Jesus Christ in our lives. We call this Christian Hope. It is one of the three "Theological Virtues" - Faith, Hope and Love, set out by Saint Paul in his First Letter to the Corinthians where he tells us:-

But for now, these three continue: faith, hope, and charity. And the greatest of these is charity." (1 Cor 13:13)

Saint Paul tells us two other very important things about hope:

" But hope is not unfounded, because the love of God is poured forth in our hearts through the Holy Spirit, who has been given to us." (Romans 5:5)

"If we have hope in Christ for this life only, then we are more miserable than all men." 1 Cor 15:19)

The prayer which immediately follows the Lord's Prayer at Mass is generally known as the "Libera nos" which means "Deliver us". It is there to emphasise the last words of the "Our Father" which are "deliver us from evil". Within that prayer we acknowledge our ever-present need for peace, freedom from sin and security, which it describes as "awaiting the blessed hope and the coming of our Saviour Jesus Christ".

It really is a wonderful prayer for Advent, isn't it? We are waiting for the coming of Jesus. When we speak of the Lord's coming, we think back to His first coming as the Babe of Bethlehem. We also look to His future coming to judge the living and the dead at the end of time. There is also a third coming though - that coming of Jesus into our lives day by day if we remember to make room for Him.

When we look back to Bethlehem we are encouraged to hope because it was there that our human family first encountered the true gentleness and generosity of God's love for us. That the Son of God should Himself be so humble as to be born in such poverty is a miracle beyond comprehension. The Divine courtesy is seen in the gentleness of the Christ Child. Who could be afraid of a baby? When we see any baby at all, even a kitten or a puppy, our heart goes out to it. St. Francis of Assisi made the first ever Christmas Crib many centuries ago, trying to share with others the loving attraction which he felt when meditating on the stable in Bethlehem. The first coming of Jesus Christ confirms us in the hope that His promise of that He will never turn away anyone coming to Him (cf. John 6:37) is a reality for us too.

Looking ahead to the Second Coming of our Lord, to judge the living and the dead, ought not cause us a lot of anxiety either, because that same gentle Jesus will be judging us. When anxious about our own track record as Christians, we might well also ponder on the 25th chapter of St. Matthew's Gospel. There we see that the the wicked have never taken time to think what harm they have done, but neither have the righteous ones any recollection of all the good they did in life. In astonishment they ask the Lord when they did these good things, and the gentle, courteous Lord reminds them that He has remembered their compassionate acts of kindness, even when they have not. One of the Saints used to pray "Lord, let me do good without knowing it."

That brings me to what I call the "Third Coming" of Jesus Christ. It might also be called the "Middle Coming" because it sits in between that first coming in Bethlehem and that last coming in Judgement. It can be a daily reality for you and me. Every day we live, Jesus is courteously and gently waiting to be invited into your life and mine.

If we let Him enter, He brings day by day that precious gift of true hope, knowing him in all his gentleness, humility and kindness: "He bids us to make our home in Him, just as he has done in us (cf. John 15:4) Of course, having Him around day by day will make us more careful about the way we live our lives, might even seem to "cramp our style", but that can only be to our benefit and that of the whole world.

I pray that you and those you love will make Jesus your welcome guest, not just on Christmas Day, but every day. This is indeed an uncertain world, and leads some to the verge of despair. Not so the true Christian, our hope is not for this life only, but for our life in Jesus Christ, and that hope will never leave us disappointed.

****

3rd Sunday of Advent   *"A witness to the Light"*

Gospel Reading John 1:6-8, 19-20

The Third Sunday of Advent is traditionally known as "Gaudete Sunday". The name comes from the opening words of today's Mass - "Gaudete" in Latin is an imperative, a command to rejoice because the Feast of Christmas is now only days away.

The Gospel reading we hear on Christmas morning consists of more opening words, this time those found close to the beginning of St. John's Gospel, his magnificent "Prologue". The second paragraph speaks of John the Baptist:

"There was a man sent by God, whose name was John. He arrived as a witness to offer testimony about the Light, so that all would believe through him. He was not the Light, but he was to offer testimony about the Light. (John 1:19-28)

Visiting Jerusalem in 1990, I was privileged to visit the Shrine of the Book in the Israel Museum, and there see for myself the Dead Sea Scrolls. These ancient documents have an interesting history, and were quite unknown till the day in 1947, when an adventurous Palestinian boy explored a cave within a cliff side at Qumran by the Dead Sea, and he made an astounding discovery - dozens of old clay jars, which contained ancient scrolls. Archaeologists spent the next ten years exploring that cave, and others nearby. They discovered more than ten thousand fragments of parchments. Among them was a copy of the Book of Isaiah a thousand years older than any previously known to exist! These writings became known as the "Dead Sea Scrolls".

The Dead Sea Scrolls were produced over the course of a century and a half by a Jewish sect called the Essenes. This was a group of devout Jews who retreated into the desert about a hundred years before Jesus was born. They were dismayed, both by the growth of paganism brought by successive foreign occupations and no less by the way in which the Temple authorities in Jerusalem had compromised and accommodated those invaders.

They settled in the barren desert on the banks of the Dead Sea, 1300 feet below Sea level. Qumran sits about 13 miles North East of Jerusalem, the same distance South West of Jericho. It is also worth a visit, but if you go don't forget your water bottle!

At Qumran, the Essenes waited for the Messiah to come and sort things out. They occupied themselves with prayer and purification, continually studying, copying and commenting on God's word. They also went through frequent baptismal rituals to symbolize their total dedication to God's will in living a life of spiritual purity.

There is widespread agreement among scripture scholars that

a link existed between John the Baptist and the Qumran community. It would seem that John had spent time there with them, later leaving the seclusion and security of the desert because he knew the Messiah's coming was imminent. His simple lifestyle, fiery preaching of the coming Messiah and baptism for the forgiveness of sins are all typical of the Essenes. There is, however, a crucial difference between John and Qumran. The Messiah John proclaimed was not a mythical future happening, but a real person - his cousin Jesus of Nazareth, the Word made flesh and living among them. John is important to Advent; although not the Light himself, he bore fearless witness to the Light, and shows us how to do the same, despite the challenges and self-sacrifice all true discipleship demands.

People came in their hundreds to look at John, listen to him, and undergo his baptism. They weren't all Jews either. Even tough Roman Legionaries from the army of occupation came to him at Jordan, and were told to stop complaining and being so greedy - clearly he was no respecter or persons. It says much of the authority of John's character that he could speak to soldiers like that without being beaten up! Without doubt, however, John's first great breakthrough happened when a delegation of priests and Levites from the Great Council of the Temple (the Sanhedrin) arrived to check him out.

Why did they come at all? In the first place,we do well to

remember something else we know about the Baptist - he wasn't just some drop-out from the Dead Sea, he was the son of one of those temple priests, Zecheriah who belonged to the prestigious "Abijah Section" of the priesthood. Even though he had clearly decided not to minister in the temple, John was still an hereditary priest. As far as the travellers from Jerusalem were concerned, John, son of Zecheriah, was "one of their own." His lifestyle distanced him from their cultured and comfortable selves - he presented himself more like one of the old-time prophets who spoke God's word to His people Israel. The Sanhedrin felt it their duty to check up on John in case he was a false prophet, remember, the Romans would leave those priests and their temple alone only as long as they knew they weren't seen as part of the resistance movement. If John was preaching revolution and armed rebellion, the Temple priests would have found themselves standing on shaky ground, hence their questions. Was John the Christ, the Anointed One, the Messiah? He firmly told them that he was not. In that case, what about Elijah? (Many devout Jews believed Elijah would return before the Christ) Again, John denied that this was the case. Was he another prophet? John replied that he was not. The delegates must have allowed themselves a little sigh of relief. John's baptism, they concluded, was symbolic only of forgiveness of sin (God alone had power to forgive sin). Then they returned to the matter in hand; John had told them who he was not, but the Sanhedrin would want more than that - if not Christ, Elijah or prophet, just who was he?

This gave John his golden opportunity to bear witness to Jesus. The good preacher does not preach himself, and good witnesses do not draw attention to themselves, so John took great care in presenting Jesus as superior to himself in every way.

John answered them by saying:
"I baptize with water. But in your midst stands one, whom you do not know. The same is he who is to come after me, who has been placed ahead of me, the laces of whose shoes I am not worthy to loosen." (John 1:26)

Rabbinic custom dictated that a disciple should do for his master anything that a servant did, excepting only removing his sandals. That was too menial a service even for a disciple to render. So John said: "One is coming whose slave I am not fit to be." John's mission was only to "prepare the way." Any greatness he possessed came from the greatness of the one whose coming he foretold. John the Baptist lived only to bear witness to Christ. Advent calls us to remember that we are Christ's witnesses today. People round us still "Walk in darkness". For some, it is the darkness of poverty and oppression. Others are deafened and blinded by the empty and temporary attractions of the world. The commercial

"Festive Season" throws into focus many who feel lonely, unwanted, rejected, and marginalized. They need us to show them that Great Light prophesied by Isaiah, the Light of Christ. Yes, Christmas is a great family feast, an enchanted celebration for children of all ages, <u>but let us remember that great human family of ours - every single one of our world's seven billion inhabitants is a child of God</u>, and Christmas is not complete unless we show real generosity to those who have nothing to give us in return.

The modern Saint, Mother Teresa of Calcutta taught that holiness consisted in "doing small things but with great love". As we prepare to celebrate Christmas and the coming of God into our lives we need also to remind ourselves that we have been called to be the means of bringing Jesus into other people's lives too.

****

4th Sunday of Advent

Gospel Reading: Luke 1:26-38

I doubt there's a Catholic Church anywhere in the world where you wouldn't find a statue or picture of Our Blessed Lady. The same could once have been said of Catholic homes, though I've noticed with regret in recent years that this is no longer so much the case. Catholics have a deep love for Our Lady and rightly so, for she is the best of all loving Mothers to us all: understanding, a ready listener, a loving consoler and a welcoming refuge in our sorrows. Not all Christians feel that same affection to Our Lady; some mistakenly think that she is a barrier to a personal love for Jesus - anything but! It is less common to find images of Our Lady in their places of worship, but Christmas at least gives her a place, for it is impossible to have a Crib without Mary. Many other figures can be spared, Kings, Shepherds, Ox and Ass - none of these is essential, but she is. On this final Sunday of Advent, we give Our Lady "Star Billing" in the Gospel as we hear again Saint Luke's wonderful account of the Annunciation.

The story is familiar, but we must not allow that very familiarity to make us indifferent to this crucial moment in our salvation history. There is a story of a famous composer conducting one of his best-known pieces which was being played by a top class orchestra. They had played it so many times that they began the piece automatically, paying scant heed to the conductor. The great man brought them to a standstill, and then said "Gentlemen, I would be obliged if you would play this piece as if you were playing it for the very first time!" We have already meditated on the Annunciation many times. This morning, however, shall we try to imagine we had never heard the story before?

"Then, in the sixth month, the Angel Gabriel was sent by God, to a city of Galilee named Nazareth, to a virgin betrothed to a man whose name was Joseph, of the house of David; and the name of the virgin was Mary." (Luke 1:26)

Miriam (which is what she would have called herself) is a simple girl, engaged to the local carpenter. Her dreams are of a good husband, a happy marriage - what young woman of her place and time could have wished for more?

Then the angel comes:

And upon entering, the Angel said to her: "Hail, full of grace. The Lord is with you. Blessed are you among women."

What does it mean, this "Full of grace"? What are her achievements, her qualifications, her possessions? What has merited God's favour? *"He has looked with favour on the humility of His handmaid" (Luke 1:48}* - her very humility means that she is radically open to the grace of God.

"The Lord is with you" those words were full of meaning to a first century Jew. In the religious stories Mary heard growing up, they were spoken to the likes of Moses, Gideon and David, great leaders one and all. Miriam is greatly troubled to hear them. Her nation is under the iron heel of Rome, and it is dangerous for anyone to stand out from the crowd.

"And when she had heard this, she was disturbed by his words, and she considered what kind of greeting this might be. And the Angel said to her: "Do not be afraid, Mary, for you have found grace with God. Behold, you shall conceive in your womb, and you shall bear a son, and you shall call his name: JESUS. He will be great, and he will be called the Son of the Most High, and the Lord God will give him the throne of David his father. And he will reign in the house of Jacob for eternity. And his kingdom shall have no end." (Luke 1:26-9)

Time and again, the Lord God had said to his people "Do not be afraid". The Hebrew people believed that God's defining characteristics were mercy and faithfulness. That expression crops up 366 times in the Bible - once for each day of every year, including leap years! Bring your own fears to God today and hear him speak in the silence of your heart: "Don't be afraid, I am by your side always".

The Angel has spoken terrifying words - a child to an unmarried mother - Son of the Most High - Throne of David - Rule the House of Jacob. All dangerous concepts, fraught with trouble.

She questions the angel: *"How shall this be done, since I do not know man?"* – she's still a virgin, how can she bear a son?

The Angel replies: *"The Holy Spirit will pass over you, and the power of the Most High will overshadow you. And because of this also, the Holy One who will be born of you shall be called the Son of God."*   *(Luke 1:35)*

Yet again, the angel speaks darkly mysterious words. The "Ruah", the Breath of God, the power of El Shaddai will "overshadow" her. The child will be called "Son of God".

But notice that he speaks not a word about the immediate problem of Mary's pregnancy! God can at times ask us to go forward in faith and be prepared to wait for answers.

He does, however, give Mary more astounding news, this time about her elderly cousin Elizabeth who has herself conceived a son! Nothing, the angel assures her, is beyond God's power.

Nothing is impossible to God - more blessed words! And a "small miracle" to prove the truth of the words, old Elizabeth is "six months gone", the old lady they believed barren is expecting a baby.

Advent is a good time to remember the "small miracles" you

have seen over the years - with God there are no "coincidences", no "accidents", nothing happens as a result of random chance. All is blessing.

Mary said, *'Behold, I am the handmaid of the Lord. Let it be done to me according to your word." And the Angel departed from her. (Luke 1:38)*

And with that, the angel departed. Just like us, Our Lady had to live her life by faith. At Bethlehem it was the shepherds who saw and heard the choir of angels, the Magi who were led by a sign in the heavens. There is no mention of any such privilege for the Mother of God that night, for her the stark reality of a cold stable, and no better cot for her new-born child than a bed of hay in a manger.

At the Presentation in the Temple, old Simeon prophesied a Sword of Sorrow which would pierce her heart. How often she is shown in Christian art standing at the foot or the cross, or in the image of the "Pieta", seated with the lifeless body of Her Son cradled in her arms.

In our devotion to Our Blessed Lady, we need to remain in touch with the reality of her life, and the world in which she lived it. Hers was no fairy-tale existence, most highly favoured though she might be. God's blessings tend to come heavily disguised, not least for the Mother of God.

Small wonder that Christian people down the ages have

instinctively draw close to her in their own "vale of tears". As Saint Bernard said, no one has ever sought her intercession, implored her help, and been left forsaken.

From one generation to the next, the Mother of God holds out her infant Son, who comes with His infinite heart full of love for each and every one of us. This is the greatest, best and most precious Christmas present of them all - as John Wesley said at the end of his life: "The best of all is that God is with us."

****

Christmas Day   *Emmanuel - God with us.*

Gospel reading John 1:1-18

The Gospel we hear at Mass of today is taken from the first chapter of Saint John's Gospel, that part usually known as the Prologue. This is a passage of scripture so very important that for centuries it was read at every single Sunday Mass. We called it "The Last Gospel" and the priest recited it in Latin at the very end of the Mass. We had two Gospels, one in the place we still have it, but another reading, always the same one, at the end of Mass. As the Last Gospel was being read we all stood, but the congregation, and especially the servers, had to keep their ears open for the words "Et Verbum caro factum est" (And the Word was made flesh) because at that point we all knelt down. Any one of you who attended Mass before the early 60's will remember that.

"The Word became flesh and he lived among us". We no longer have a Last Gospel, but those words still have such significance that they stand at the very summit of our Christmas Season. They are, dare I say, more central to the meaning of Christmas than many of the other themes and images we so enjoy. When Saint John speaks of the Incarnation, the Word made flesh, there is no star, no angels, no stable, no shepherds, no Magi, no ox, no ass - just that simple yet all-important proclamation, **Word made flesh and**

living with us.

In the original Greek text of Saint John's Gospel, the expression we translate as "dwelt amongst us" in fact means "he pitched his tent with us". And that is the thought I want you all to take from this Mass and into your Christmas celebrations. If you can find time, even ten seconds of quiet, you can repeat those words to yourself "The Word was made flesh, and pitched his tent with us."

The Vatican Council encouraged us to think of the Church as "God's pilgrim people". We are all of us on a journey, which started in the same place and will finish in the same place. In between the beginning and the end, however, there is an awful lot of space to travel, explore, wander into, and get lost in! Where are you on your pilgrimage, I wonder? This much we all have in common, that none of us can ever choose to stay where we are - time marches on, and so must we!

There is precious little in this life that we can rely on, but there is one firm foundation of Christian hope, and that is that the Love which came down on earth two millennia ago is still here on earth. Better still, that Love Incarnate, that Word made flesh, is never far away from you. You and I may very well pitch our moving tents in different places tonight, but we can each of us be sure that, wherever we stop, the Lord Jesus stays right by our side. The proclamation of Christmas is "Love came down at Christmas" to be sure, but it didn't end there, and we should learn to say "Love stays with me every day, every night of my life" That's what remains when everything else associated with Christmas is taken away. It is the very heart of Christmas.

One last thought. There is a Hebrew word we often hear in Advent, and that is the word "Emmanuel", which we mostly translate as "God with us", but Hebrew has a tiny vocabulary and one word generally means several different things. The "El" at the end of the word always denotes God. The "Emmanu", however, has many meanings, one of them is "To accompany on a journey". <u>God is always with you, wherever life may lead you</u>. Don't ever despair in any situation. Jesus is with you, Jesus journeys with you. He is Emmanuel, Word made flesh, God who walks beside you wherever you go, and who rests beside you wherever lay down your head.

May the Joy of Christ, the Love of Christ and the Peace of Christ be yours this day, and for ever!

****

The Feast of the Holy Family

Gospel reading: Luke 2:22-40

There is an old Latin proverb which runs "Omnis analogia claudicat". This is often, and very badly, translated as "Comparisons are odious". It doesn't actually mean that, and common sense alone should teach us that comparisons can be far from hateful, but very beneficial. What the Latin actually means is "Every analogy is lame". Analogy is the likening of one thing to another which differs from it, as when we speak of the "foot of a mountain". The foot of a mountain, and the foot of a human person are totally different, but the position of your foot, and the bottom of a high mountain are both the lowest part, so although you know that Mount Everest doesn't stand on a huge pair of boots, you still understand the word.

When we talk about God, and the things of God, we are nearly always speaking analogously, and that is very much the case when it comes to **family**. We speak of "God our Father", "Jesus our Brother" and of "Mother Church". We call priests "Father", and our fellow-Christians as "Brothers and Sisters".

This particular analogy also "limps" quite often. Someone whose experience of parenthood was one of neglect, rejection or abuse may well be repelled to think of God and Church in terms of "Father and Mother". People who have seen hypocrisy, selfishness and dishonesty in those who call themselves "Christian" may not like the idea of kinship with such people.

The reality of family life is often far from the ideal, isn't it? Families sometimes work much better when their members are apart. "Absence" they say "makes the heart grow fonder". Many a comedian's stock in trade has been jokes about family. One of my favourites is the following conversation between a mother and her miserable teenage son:

"What's the matter with you?"
"I'm homesick."
"But this *is* your home."
"Yeah, and I'm *sick* of it!"

The first Sunday after Christmas is celebrated as the Feast of the Holy Family. Our readings and prayers in this Mass put before us the example of Jesus, Mary and Joseph, encouraging us to reflect on God's plan for our own family living.

Pope Francis teaches us how to understand the true meaning of Christian family life in the Lord:

"To understand the family today we need to enter into the mystery of the family of Nazareth, into its quiet daily life, not unlike that of most families, with their problems and their simple joys, a life marked by serene patience amid adversity, respect for others, a humility which is freeing and which

flowers in service, a life of fraternity rooted in the sense that we are all members of one body." (Feast of the Holy Family, December 2018)

The Holy Father speaks practical words of wisdom from experience. His many years of pastoral care in South America mean that he does not wish us to see the Holy Family as a collection of "plaster saints", lovely to look at but a million miles from our own experience of family life. Problem-free, perpetually smiling families may be the stuff of television advertisements, such a false portrayal of the Holy Family, however, could only ever be a discouragement to the rest of us. The Holy Family is a real family, not a fairy tale. As such, it has much to teach us today.

First of all, there is the fundamental truth that marriage and family life are a <u>Vocation</u>. Every family is called to make visible and communicate the life and love of Christ. We do this by recognising Christ present in those with whom we live, and welcoming Christ in those who come into our homes. Pope Francis has encouraged us to "listen to Him, speak with Him, take care of Him, protect Him and grow with Him, and in this way improve the world." (ibid)

In practical terms, the weeks of Advent have given us many opportunities to reflect upon the lives and characters of Mary and Joseph. Parents have such wonderful examples to follow in caring for the children God gives them. We have also seen them responding to God's will positively and generously in times of great personal difficulty and uncertainty. Both Mary and Joseph more than once find themselves facing events which they had never expected. They may have been thwarted in their own personal plans and expectations of married life, but both have the faith and courage to see that this is not God giving them less, but far, far more.

One of the really important lessons good parents try hard to teach their children is not to respond immediately to every stimulus, circumstance or inclination, but to consider the possible consequences of our actions. Every choice, every action, every decision we make will have consequences, good or ill, for ourselves for other people, and for our world. As human beings, we seldom see the future at all clearly - who could have foreseen a century ago to untold environmental damage or the aerosol or the internal combustion engine? One of the scientists who worked to develop the atom bomb was appalled when he saw the weapon in action. ""Now," he exclaimed "I am become death!". It's not, however, only the bad consequences we can't see - the good and positive outcomes are mostly lost on us too.

For a young woman to find herself expecting a baby before marriage, for her intended to know that the child is not his. These are challenging   circumstances, and could have resulted in Mary being stoned to death as an adulteress. Mary and Joseph, however, made their own will subject to God's and so, as Saint Matthew opened his Gospel last Sunday: *"Now the birth of Jesus Christ took place in this way"*. To be stuck in an overcrowded, unfamiliar town, the baby's birth expected any moment, no room at the inn, reduced to giving birth in a stable - again, rather bad luck at first sight, and very humiliating. Yet the consequences of that reach down even into our own time, with millions of Christmas Cribs in churches, market places and homes the world over because that poor, humble child of Bethlehem is accessible to every human person. *"Divine providence would have Jesus born in a stable, expressing his solidarity with the lowly and identifying with all those who suffer, who weep, who suffer any kind of injustice."* (Pope Francis, op .cit.)

Again, nobody chooses to become a homeless, stateless, refugee - a stranger among strangers, and we all do well to remember that, don't we? Herod's jealous anger and institutionalised infanticide force the Holy Family to hit the road to Egypt. The consequences of that are that Christian hearts and homes have been open to refugees for centuries, and please God will remain so.

God did not choose to enter our world "trailing clouds of glory". Neither did He choose to live a life of privilege, honour and wealth. Perhaps this gives us a true picture of the true worthlessness of all three in the eternal scheme of things. Incredibly, God chose to entrust Himself and His work of redemption to the care of a human family. He could do this because that family was founded on love and not distracted with material wealth or aspirations. It was a family at whose heart was a radical denial of self and openness to Divine providence. Mary and Joseph found God in hard places and unpromising circumstances. Saint Ignatius of Loyola said that the heart of Christian spirituality is "To find God in all things".

Family life is not easy. You and your families walk a hard road, but it is at least a well-trodden path. You do not walk that path alone and in darkness either. Jesus, Mary and Joseph walk right by your side, and Jesus is the Light of the World.

The Holy Family of Nazareth shows our families how to be holy and how to help others be holy. The witness of families who answer God's call, who open the doors of their hearts, reaches far beyond the walls of their home. It speaks the Gospel by their example to their extended family, to neighbours, to friends, to schoolmates, to everyone. It brings Christ to the world. Jesus tells us to go out to all the world, proclaiming the good news of the Gospel. Christian family life does just that.

****

Epiphany   *The two journeys of the Magi*

Gospel reading Matthew 2:1-12

The beautiful Crib will soon be taken down and stored away until next Christmas. The Feast of the Epiphany brings our Christmas celebrations to an end. At the very last moment, three more figures put in their appearance, one might say "late and out of breath". The latecomers are, of course, the Magi, also known as Kings and Wise Men. Their story occupies just eleven verses of Saint Matthew's Gospel. That apart, they are never referred to at all. Matthew doesn't even tell us how many there were (the number three is deduced from the gifts they brought, assuming they brought one each). These mysterious figures, however, have always figured large in the Christmas story, and, judging from the number of Christmas cards I still receive with the Magi on them, that is not going to change any time soon!

The word "Epiphany" comes from the Greek for "Manifestation" (Showing). When the Magi came to Bethlehem, they were the first Gentiles (Non-Jewish people) to see the new-born Son of God. The Old Testament abounds with promises that God would make Himself known to "The Nations" (The Gentiles) [Micah 4:2, Psalm 67:2, Psalm 22:27, Isaiah 49:6, Zecheriah 8:22, and many more!]. The visit of the Magi marked the fulfilment of that promise. The three foreign visitors brought with them precious and prophetic gifts:

Frankincense to honour Christ as true God, Gold to proclaim Him as Universal King, and Myrrh to foretell the terrible suffering and death He would endure as Redeemer of the world.

This morning, I would like to share with you just two further thoughts about the Magi. They made, not one but two journeys, one to Bethlehem, and another back home, in all likelihood to Babylon.

In considering the first journey they made, we have to bear in mind that they travelled a long way - "*Field and fountain, moor and mountain*" as the carol says. They would also have crossed a significant tract of desert. On that journey, they didn't really know where they were going, or what they would find when they got there. The motive for their journey was their quite erroneous belief in astrology, the power of stars to govern our lives. They thought they had seen something special in the course of their star-gazing, and set off on a journey of discovery.

They not only suffered from superstition, they were also inclined (and aren't most of us?) to jump to conclusions on the basis of prejudice. This brought them first of all to the wrong place entirely, the palace of King Herod - where else would a King be born? Herod had a dreadful reputation far and wide. He was known to have murdered several members of his own family in case they challenged his authority. According to the later Roman writer Macrobius, even the Roman Emperor Augustus knew his reputation and observed "It is better to be Herod's pig than his son!" (Saturnalia II.XI). The Magi should have known this - what were they thinking of, blundering into Herod's palace? This thoughtless lack of judgement set in motion the wheels of the Massacre of the Holy Innocents. Wise Men? I wonder!

Like the Magi, we too have made our own journey to the Crib this Christmas. Some of us have travelled a long way. The longer our journey, the more mistakes we are likely to have made, though few can have been as catastrophic as telling the jealous and homicidal Herod that a new king was born in his backyard. Importantly, the Magi did not let this great blunder deter them. They could not undo the damage they had caused, but they were wise in accepting that fact and continuing their quest. The remembrance of past misdeeds, both those we have caused and those we have suffered, can become a terrible burden in the spiritual life. Do you remember Dickens' "A Christmas Carol"? Poor Jacob Marley's ghost appeared dragging along heavy cash boxes which were chained to him. It is possible for us to be the same - chained to the burden of a past we cannot change. An ancient Chinese sage called Lao Tsu said "*If you live in the past, you will be sad*". To be sure, we all have to live <u>with</u> our past, but we don't need to live <u>in</u> it. If you are burdened by your past today, take a quiet moment in the presence of Our Lord in church this morning. In the Gospels, Jesus has a special greeting for the repentant He meets: "Go in peace, your sins are forgiven".

Faithful to their journey, those Magi found Jesus with Our Blessed Lady and Saint Joseph. The Angels are kept very busy by Saint Matthew and Saint Luke in telling us of the birth of Jesus. One of those hard-working Angels is sent to warn the Magi to steer clear of Herod on the way home. Wisely, they heed the warning and find another way back - they don't just go away the same as they arrived.

We ourselves should not say goodbye to the Christmas crib unchanged either. There is another of Lao Tsu's sayings that warns against living for tomorrow: "*If you live in the future, you will be fearful. Only if you live in the present will you be at peace*" Shall we try to apply those words to ourselves, to accept the precious gift of each "today" with gratitude and use IT as well as we can?

Not all wisdom, of course, comes from the ancient Chinese. The Church has produced many wise men and women of her own. One of these is Saint Augustine, who advised: *"Leave the past to God's mercy, the present to His love, and the future to His providence."* May God grant us the wisdom to live in the present, in His presence, this New Year!

****

Feast of the Baptism of Our Lord

Gospel reading: Mark 1:7-11

Last Sunday, we celebrated the Feast of the Epiphany, and the Magi made their all-too-brief appearance in the crib. In most parishes, the crib is dismantled after "Twelfth Night", when the Christmas decorations come down. In Saint Mary's Derby (my very first appointment as a priest) they followed the more ancient English Catholic practice of leaving the crib in place until Candlemas. This, of course, gave the Magi much more exposure, but that wasn't the reason. There are two very good reasons for leaving the crib in place - the first is that it isn't really a "Christmas decoration" like the tree, the holly and the mistletoe, relics of the pagan Midwinter festival. No, the crib is entirely Christian in origin, and is really a visual aid to give people a background to the coming of God made man into our world. The second reason is that the liturgical celebration of the Epiphany does not end on 6th January. The Church Fathers taught that the "manifestation" of Jesus Christ happened in three stages, the first being the visit of the Magi, the second the Baptism of Our Lord, and the third His first miracle, changing water into wine during the wedding at Cana in Galilee.

This three-stage Epiphany was very much in William Wordsworth's mind when he wrote his lovely hymn "Songs of Thankfulness and Praise", in which he speaks of Jesus "manifested by a star to the sages from afar", then goes on to say "manifest at Jordan stream, prophet, priest and king supreme", and finally "manifest in power divine, changing water into wine". The real Christmas story does not end when the crib goes back into the cupboard!

Today we celebrate that second stage of that Epiphany, the manifestation of Our Lord's divinity. The significance of the event is made very clear by the fact that all four Gospels tell of the day, when Jesus came to Jordan, where his cousin John was baptising. Other than the Baptism of Jesus, only the events of the first Easter are to be found in all four Gospels. Indeed, neither Saint Mark nor Saint John include the Nativity at Bethlehem at all, so scripturally Our Lord's Baptism is a highly significant event.

I want to spend a few minutes this morning thinking about Saint Mark's account, today's Gospel. Mark tells the story in a very clear way, in just two short paragraphs, speaking first of Our Lord's relationship with the human race, and then of the relationship with God our Father which the human race may have through Jesus Christ.

Let's consider that first paragraph. Jesus came from Galilee to Jordan, where John was baptising. Crowds of ordinary folk came to hear the Baptist preach and then to be immersed in the river as a sign of sorrow for their sins. Their public admission of sin perhaps sits uncomfortably on the shoulders of twenty-first century men and women. Our insurers and legal advisers so often urge us NOT TO ADMIT THAT ANYTHING WAS OUR FAULT! Any admission of fault, responsibility or sin on one's own part is likely to have financial consequences in these litigious times. No, the fault must always rest with another - wrongdoing is something that HAPPENS TO me, never something DONE BY me! We begin each Mass by acknowledging our sins "through my fault, through my fault, through my most grievous fault", but dare we say that anywhere except in Church? The people who crowded around John knew they had sinned, they admitted as much, and they wanted to make a fresh start. Jesus came and stood with them. He had not come to call the righteous, but sinners. He saw our human sin as a sickness which He alone could heal. John's baptism was a real sign of repentance, but it was no more than a symbol and couldn't forgive sin. Jesus came to bring the gifts of Baptism and the Holy Spirit for true forgiveness.

It was the Father's will that Jesus should be baptised by John that day. Jesus, entirely without sin, was to identify Himself completely with those who were in sin. Saint Paul describes this so well in his Second Letter to the people in Corinth where he says: *"For our sake he made him who knew no sin to be sin, that in him we might become the righteousness of God"* (5:21). When Jesus went freely to the cross, he bore with him all the world's sin, past present and to come, died and rose from the dead so that we might all be given the chance to have our sins forgiven. What a gift we celebrate today!

Saint Mark goes on to describe the moment when Jesus came out of the water, the Holy Spirit coming down on Him in the form of a dove, and the Father's voice heard saying *"You are my beloved Son, in you I am well pleased."* (Mark 1:11} The mystery of the Holy Trinity was manifested on the day Jesus was baptised - another great gift to celebrate.

"You are my child, my beloved child, I am well pleased with you" The Father speaks those selfsame words to each and every one of us on the day we are baptised. This is what the Father says to you and me when he sees us at Mass together today - this is what the Father says when you pray, this is what He says every instant of your Christian life: "I LOVE YOU".

Pause for a moment right now, and hear the Father say those words to YOU.......... When Jesus came to save us, it was not due to any merits on the part of humanity. He came to fulfil the Father's will, and to teach us the true meaning of love. In His incarnation Jesus brings hope to a world darkened by sin. I had the privilege of being ordained a priest in a coastal parish dedicated to Our Lady Star of the Sea. May her immaculate Star shine on you and yours throughout the coming year.

Second Sunday "Per Annum"   *"I heard the cat "Miaow"!*

I like to think of today's Gospel as "A Symphony in Four Movements". Four distinct and yet closely associated things take place.

1. John the Baptist identifies, and bears witness to, Jesus the "Lamb of God".

2. Andrew and his companion follow after Jesus, but hesitantly and at a distance.

3. Jesus stops, turns round, and invites the two to come with Him.

4. Simon is brought by Andrew to Jesus next day, and Jesus tells him that he is to be Peter, the Rock on which the Church will be built.

This gives me just two or three minutes for each of them!

1. Less than a month ago, on the Third Sunday of Advent, I devoted the whole homily to John the Baptist, so he should still be fresh in your minds. I'm sure you remember how he said he was there to prepare a way for the Lord, whose sandals he was not worthy to unfasten. Sometimes, people who speak humbly do not like to behave in the same way. John, however, was as humble in his actions as his words. When Jesus came, John pointed Him out as "Lamb of God" and sent his disciples to Him. John was an important figure at that time. Outspoken people often make important enemies

and John was no exception. His safety lay in the strength of his following. Sending his disciples away would leave John very vulnerable, especially to King Herod who feared him, and Queen Herodias who hated him. John was a very faithful witness to Christ. He stood his ground, whatever people thought or said. He was quite willing to yield in humility before Jesus, to see his own power and popularity wane, to put himself in harm's way, and all for the sake of Jesus. Small wonder that Our Lord spoke of John with such warmth and appreciation: *"For I say to you, among those born of women no one is greater than John the Baptist."* (Matthew 11:11, Luke 7:28)

2. John sends Andrew and his unnamed companion after Jesus who is passing by. They follow, but hesitantly and at a distance. Just who this Jesus is, what He will ask of them, where he may lead them, they do not know. Our own faith journey is so very like that. Some years ago, there was a debate between two famous philosophers, one an atheist, the other a believer. The unbeliever started the ball rolling by saying: "As far as I can tell, what you call "faith" is like a blind man in a dark cellar, trying to find a black cat that isn't there!". The Christian replied "Yes, it's very much like that for me as a believer - except that I once heard the cat 'miaow'!" As St. Paul says, *"We walk by means of faith, not by sight"*. (2 Corinthians 5:7)

3. Importantly though, God does not leave us to flounder on as best we can. Andrew and his friend soon discover this: Jesus stops, turns round, and speaks to them. *"What do you want?"*. Their reply is profound in its simplicity: *"Rabbi, where do you live?"*. Why did they ask the question? Because, if they were to learn from him, they would need to know where to find him next day. Jesus replies: *"Come and see!"*. He invites them to walk, not behind Him, but with Him - to join Him in a journey which will involve having "no fixed abode" and lead them to places they would not otherwise have dreamt of visiting, and meeting people they wouldn't otherwise have dreamt of speaking to. They are to join Him in an uncertain journey of discovery for which there is no road map. They would have to walk by faith, not by sight.

4. The following day, Andrew goes again in search of Jesus. This time he takes his brother Peter with him. It is greatly to Saint Andrew's credit that he is the man responsible for introducing the first Pope to the Founder of Christianity. Jesus immediately discerns far more in Simon than the latter ever saw in himself. Jesus names him the Rock on which He will build His Church. Those words must have meant nothing to Saint Peter at that first meeting, but he too would journey with Jesus in faith, and come to understand his vocation on the way, but not till after quite a few ups and downs!

WITH HIM ...IN HIM

This Gospel invites us to reflect upon the faith we share. Where did it come from? We learned about Jesus from inspiring people just like John the Baptist - priests, sisters, teachers. We learned also from the prayerful example of parents, godparents, grandparents, and others. We have been supported along our own journey by those who have accompanied us down the years. But none of these actually gave us our faith. That came to us as the gracious and personal gift of God alone, a gift we can never give to others, dearly as we would love to. At the moment the gift was given, Jesus himself turned to each of us and called us by name to walk with Him.

Thank God for the gift of faith, for that precious moment when Jesus spoke within your own soul and said "Follow me". Thank God for those who by word, example and companionship have supported you on the journey. Their cherished memory, their presence with us, is a great comfort to us, blind in a dark cellar looking for a black cat, but neither they, nor we, would continue the journey but for our own personal encounter with Jesus. We journey on by faith and not by sight, confident that the journey will not end in failure. We too, thank God, have "heard the cat 'miaow'!"

****

<u>3rd Sunday "Per Annum"</u>   *Picturing the Word of God.*

Our Holy Father Pope Francis has asked us to observe this Sunday as "Sunday of the Word of God". Saint Jerome tells us "Ignorance of the Scriptures is ignorance of Christ". We are called to make ourselves ever more familiar with God's Word, this year especially Saint Mark's Gospel. There is a practice to help us read and hear the Word more effectively, or at least I've found it so. Saint Ignatius Loyola called it "Composition of Place", and it simply means forming mental pictures of the people, events and places we have read about. This became a great deal easier for me after a pilgrimage to the Holy Land more than thirty years ago.

I cherish memories of the Sea of Galilee, where the unchanged landscape provides us with the backdrop for today's Gospel story. The Sea of Galilee, sometimes called Tiberius or Gennesaret, is really a lake, but a very large one indeed, 13 miles long and 8 miles across. Standing on the stony banks, with water lapping gently at your feet, even to this day you will still see fisherman with small boats going out over the water, just as Peter and his companions did. When the fishing is over, they bring their nets and wash them clean at a place called in Aramaic "Ein sheva", in Greek Επταπήγωνο "Heptapegon", later shortened to "Tabgha" where seven streams run into the lake. Many scripture scholars have situated the call of the Apostles there. We might wonder why Jesus chose to call those first Apostles exactly in that place. One reason is again explained by the location. Capernaum was not only a bustling fishing village but also stood at a crossroads between the Greek-influenced cities to the east and the westward Jewish towns and settlements. The great nations to the north and south, Syria and Egypt had made extensive use of the road there, for commercial, diplomatic and at times military purposes. There were always plenty of Roman soldiers around too. Unsurprisingly, the area was known to the Jewish people as "Galilee of the Nations" - for the Jews the "Nations" (Ha Goyim) meant the Gentiles, the foreign, non-Jewish people, those who were not part of God's chosen people. In basing Himself in Capernaum and spending so much of his time ministering in Galilee, and Gentile areas to the south and on the far side of the River Jordan, Jesus gave a clear and practical demonstration that all people are God's chosen ones.

We have heard the Bible stories so many times now that there is always the danger that they lose their freshness and their ability to surprise us. It has been said that many Christians experience the Gospel stories like old, well-worn coins, with the image and writing on them almost rubbed away by the passage of years. Maybe it felt a little bit like that for you when listening to the Gospel this morning. In fact, Saint Matthew tells us a strange and rather unsettling story. Can you imagine four men simply walking away from everything, their jobs, families, responsibilities, their entire way of life, just because a passing carpenter speaks a few words to them?

At that time in the Holy Land, just as in many eastern countries to this day, custom demanded that the pupils chose the teacher, the Rabbi did not choose his own disciples. In calling those fishermen (and ourselves for that matter) the Lord never allows Himself to be limited by our human customs, standards or expectations. In our relationship with God, the only thing we can be really certain of is that things never turn out the way we expect. We never get what we hoped and prayed for, planned or anticipated, and God always ends up giving us far more than we could ever imagine!

The call to become "fishers of men" is again so familiar as to have lost all of its impact. This effect is the greater because of the way that our Lord's words, reported by Saint Matthew in Greek, have been translated into English. There is a distinction in the Greek language between "Anthropos", which means every human person, male or female, and "Andros" which denotes males only. Matthew uses the first word - all humanity. When Jesus says "follow me", there is no distinction between male or female, young or old, black or white, rich or poor, educated or not. As Saint Paul tells us *"You are all one in Christ Jesus"* (Gal 3:28)

The last point to ponder for this week is in that very

expression: "Fishers of Men". It is to be found nowhere in the Old Testament or other writings - Jesus used it first. The image of discipleship which Jesus puts before Peter and his companions is one which is drawn immediately from their own experience of life. Again and again in the Gospels we find Jesus doing this. His images are drawn from nature, the weather, our human occupations and recreations. When God calls us, He calls us **as we are** and **where we are.** There may be times when we are tempted to believe that our own family circumstances, temperament, and personal failings are a barrier to discipleship. Far from it! When Jesus looks at you today, He sees in you all of the gifts and experience needed to be a true and effective disciple.

Pause from time to time in the week ahead, close your eyes, try to picture that scene on the shores of Galilee. Imagine yourself as one of those the Master approaches. He looks at you with infinite love and says "Follow me". What will your response be?

****

4th Sunday "Per Annum" *Many opinions, one truth!*

Saint Mark tells us, not once but twice, in today's short Gospel reading that people were amazed by the way Jesus taught. He did not instruct them in the customary fashion, He taught with authority. What does Mark mean by this? To understand why the teaching of Jesus was not like that of the synagogue Scribes, we must first be clear what a synagogue was in those days, and how the Scribes did teach.

The synagogue was not a place for sacrifice or worship, but a place to study and learn God's Law. If we think for a moment about the history of Israel, we will see that the great Jerusalem Temple was not built until the time of King Solomon. Before that, the Ark of the Covenant was kept in a tent which moved from place to place. There were a variety of shrines throughout the land of Israel where God was worshipped. It was King David, Solomon's father, who brought the Ark of the Covenant into the city of Jerusalem as he tried to cement together the alliance of the tribes into one great nation. From the time the temple was built, tremendous efforts were made to stop worship and sacrifice being offered to the God of Israel anywhere at all in the land apart from Jerusalem itself. This was never entirely successful, not least because Solomon's son Rehoboam managed to antagonise the northern tribes so much that they broke away and formed their own independent Northern Kingdom in Samaria, using the older northern shrines for worship and sacrifice. Then came the successive invasions of both northern and southern kingdoms with the destruction of the Jerusalem temple and the exile of a large proportion of the population to Babylon. It was at this time that the synagogues came into being. They provided the exiled and scattered Jewish people with a means of staying in touch with the faith of their fathers, and teaching that same faith to their children. They had nowhere to offer sacrifice or temple worship. This was not, however a complete disaster because the Jewish people believed that <u>the most important element of their faith was the Law which God had given to Moses on Mount Sinai, the Ten Commandments</u>. In the synagogue the Law could be proclaimed, taught and also applied to their changed and changing circumstances. The perfection of the Law of God is celebrated In Psalm 19:8-9) where we read:

"The Law of the Lord is perfect, it revives the soul; the decrees of the Lord are steadfast, they give wisdom to the simple. The precepts of the Lord are right, they gladden the heart; the command of the Lord is clear, it gives light to the eyes."

Because they believed that, it followed for them that the Law would be able to govern every aspect of their lives. Each Sabbath small communities would come together to hear and consider the Law. Their learned scholars, the scribes and rabbis spent a great deal of time in applying those Ten Commandments to every possible circumstance and situation.

This, of course involved a lot of debate and disagreement. It was sometimes said that where you found five rabbis, you would be sure to find six different opinions!

The years of exile ended, the remnant of the Judean exiles returned to their ruined city and temple. The reconstruction of both took many years, and during that time the influence of the synagogues in local communities continued to grow, as did the number of laws which were derived from the original Ten Commandments. By the time of our Lord there were more than 600 of them. As well as these 600 laws, there was also a vast accumulation of "case law" from the opinions of different scholars down the years. This was not written down, competent scribes were supposed to carry it all in their memory. It used to be said that a good scribe was like a deep, cement-lined well from which not one drop of water leaked away. When the scribes and rabbis were dealing with questions regarding belief and practice of Jewish people, they did not express their own opinions, but rather were expected to quote and compare the teachings of the great scholars of former years, even though they might contradict one another. A very good example of this kind of Rabbinic teaching can be seen in the musical "Fiddler on the Roof". If you have seen the film or stage show, you will perhaps remember that the milkman Tevye has a sung monologue which he repeats as he tries to come to terms with the behaviour of his daughters, none of whom seem to want to marry people he would consider suitable. Tevye muses "On the one hand... then on the other hand.... then on another..." and so on. In the same way, a Scribe would have said "On the one hand, Rabbi Shammai says this, on the other hand, Rabbi Hillel says that, and then again, Rabbi Eliakim differs from them both....". The one thing a scribe or rabbi must never do was to express an opinion of his own. I was told of a scripture scholar who remarked, having seen the film of "Fiddler on the Roof": "That Tevye, he'd have made a good Scribe!"

Jesus impressed the little congregation in Capharnaum that day because he **did** speak on His own authority. He did not teach like the scribes with constant and often confusing references to ancient authorities. He was his own authority. We will see this again when we come to consider the Sermon on the Mount. It also helps us to understand what was going on in the Gospels when the Scribes and Pharisees keep asking Jesus "By whose authority do you teach?" As a Rabbi, Jesus was something completely new. His teaching was new, and authoritative. It was not a question of there being several valid answers. There might be a dozen opinions, but there can be only one truth, and that Truth is the person of Jesus Himself, who said "I am the Way, and the Truth and the Life". (John 14:6)

We are all of us entitled to form our own opinion, but we are not entitled to form our own truth - there can be only one truth.

<u>Jesus is that Truth</u>, and He has gifted the Catholic Church with the authority of that truth when teaching on matters of faith and morality. In our world today, there are seven billion people, and probably about as many opinions. It can be very, very confusing. Sometimes people try to sort out their own "truth", sometimes, like Pontius Pilate, they doubt whether there is really any truth at all. The Good News of Jesus Christ is that yes, there is one truth, a truth which liberates the human mind, heart and spirit. Apart from God, says the 'Imitation of Christ', "all is rough and restless" (Book 4, Chapter 2) In the midst of the seething turmoil of opinion, half-truth, fake news, spin and confusion of our world today, Jesus invites us:

"Come to me, all you who labour and have been burdened, and I will refresh you." (Matthew 11:28)

****

5th Sunday "Per Annum"   Peter's Humility

Gospel reading: Mark 1:29-39

There is a rather strange looking church in Capharnaum on the banks of Galilee. It is the Church of the House of Saint Peter. At first sight it looks like something out of science fiction, held above the ground on steel legs. Once inside there is a further surprise, for a good deal of the floor on which you walk is made of glass! It is, of course, very strong armoured glass, and is there so that pilgrims can see what lies beneath. There are the remains of two buildings to be seen, a Byzantine church dating back to the time of King Arthur, and as if that wasn't old enough, that old, old church was built on another, a simple "courtyard house" two thousand years old. On the walls of this ancient house there are many scratched graffiti. They are mostly prayers for the intercession of Saint Peter, and are written in Latin, Greek, Hebrew, Aramaic and Syriac, made by pilgrims visiting that place less than a century after Our Lord's ministry in Galilee. The evidence of archaeology and the witness of those early carvings are compelling, and eminent scholars, historians and archaeologists agree that this really is the House of Peter we read about in the Gospels, Our Lord's "headquarters" during his ministry in the North of Palestine..

According to Saint Mark (1:16) Peter was one of the four first disciples of Jesus. It was customary for a rabbi to have five disciples, so a fifth, identified by Mark as Levi the son of Alphaeus (2:13) was soon added. In the following chapter, Mark names all twelve Apostles, showing that Jesus was not just one among the hundreds of rabbis in the land, but that He had a new and more far-reaching Mission, to all twelve Tribes of Israel. Only two of the tribes had survived the centuries of warfare and exile intact. The remnants of the "Lost Tribes" had settled outside of Israel, in Egypt, Babylon, Syria, and dozens of other places. The choice of the "Twelve" signalled that Jesus of Nazareth was not there to be a "National Messiah" either. His Good News was for all the world!

Reading the Gospels makes it possible for us to accompany Peter on his spiritual journey. Jesus called him on an ordinary working day when Simon, as he was known then, and his companions were busy with their boat and nets. Last weekend, we found Jesus visiting the Capernaum synagogue, curing a demoniac and impressing the people with His authoritative teaching. Today, we heard of more cures - Simon's Mother-in-Law, then the crowds of sick people drawn from the immediate neighbourhood.

Our Lord must have been very tired at the end of that busy Sabbath - hardly a "Day of Rest" for Him! Nevertheless, He is up very early on the Monday morning, and at prayer. When Simon and his companions find Him, He tells them that it's now time to move on and proclaim the Good News further afield.

Saint Mark's Gospel is far and away the shortest of the four Gospels. It's also an exciting read, because Mark drives the action forwards at breakneck speed. The word "immediately" occurs 32 times in the Gospels, and sixteen of those occurrences are in Mark alone! Do try to sit down and read it through nonstop. It will take less than two hours, and will really help you throughout the coming months to fit the various episodes into the whole picture.

Saint Mark's was the first Gospel to be set down in writing in about 70AD, within a generation of the first Easter. The author has, from the earliest days of Christianity, been identified as John Mark, a companion of those first apostles. John is a Hebrew name, Mark a Roman one - it was very common for people in the Middle East to have two names in those days. When Saint Peter travelled to Rome itself, to proclaim the Good News there, John Mark accompanied him.

Late in the 3rd Century, Saint Eusebius of Vercelli wrote his *History of the Church (tr. Arthur Cushman, pub. Eerdmans 1890)* where he gives some background to Mark's Gospel:

"And when the divine word had made its home among them....so greatly did the splendour of piety illumine the minds of Peter's hearers that they were not satisfied with hearing

once only and were not content with the unwritten teaching of the divine Gospel, but with all sorts of entreaties they besought Mark, a follower of Peter, and the one whose Gospel is extant, that he would leave them a written monument of the doctrine which had been orally communicated to them. Nor did they cease until they had prevailed with the man, and had thus become the occasion of the written Gospel which bears the name of Mark. And they say that Peter, when he had learned through a revelation of the Spirit of that which had been done, was pleased with the zeal of the men, and that the work obtained the sanction of his authority for the purpose of being used in the churches." (Chapter 2:15)

St. Peter gave Mark the first-hand account of "all that Jesus said and did" and the Holy Spirit inspired Mark to put it in writing. So, as we read the Gospel of Mark we are reading the oral teaching of the great Apostle Peter himself.

In each of the other Gospels Peter holds a place of great prominence (walking on water, given the keys, renamed "Rock", appointed shepherd, etc.) but none of this is found in Peter's own preaching. Mark tells only of Peter's weaknesses and failures. This gives us an engaging insight into the character of our first Pope.

Peter is a humble man. Others may promote his unique

authority, but Peter, like John the Baptist, is content to "decrease" so that Jesus may "increase". He clearly understands that it is not "all about Peter" - he is anxious that people should remain focused on the message proclaimed, not the man proclaiming it. Some have seen in Mark's Gospel a sign that Peter and the Eleven were not of any great importance to the first Christians, but nothing could be further from the truth. What Mark does teach us, however, is that Peter and his companions were not very important IN THEIR OWN EYES, which is a very different story. The success of those first missionaries was due to the fact that they preached Jesus Christ, not themselves. In revealing their own weakness and failures, they proclaimed the love and mercy of God, made visible in Jesus Christ.

Let us pray that their lesson of humility is not lost on those who proclaim the Good News today.

****

6th Sunday "Per Annum"   *"Jesus felt compassion"*

Gospel reading: Mark 1:40-45

During the Covid pandemic of 2020, we had to get used to "Social Distancing". That was not the first time it had been needed though. In past centuries, isolation of (and from) the sick was the only means known to fight against epidemics of infection. I live in Derbyshire, where we honour the heroic 17th Century villagers of Eyam, who put themselves into "Lockdown" at the first sign of the bubonic plague in their village. Many of them died, but the dreaded disease spread no further. In towns and cities where there were outbreaks of the plague, the sick and their families were shut up in their own homes to die or recover, a Red Cross painted on the door, with the words "Lord, have mercy on us".

At Oscott College, where I spent six very happy years studying for the priesthood, the Georgian Chapel had a small unglazed window high up on an interior wall above the pulpit. That aperture opened into the college infirmary. There were several very nasty infections around in the college's early years, with scarlet fever a great killer. Sick students were isolated in the infirmary, away from the rest of the college. The opening into the chapel meant that they were able to hear Mass, Benediction and homilies, and even get a whiff of incense. It was an act of kindness.

An even nastier disease in the Middle Ages was leprosy. It was widespread even in The British Isles. Ancient churches up and down the country also have small windows in the wall. Often glazed over now, they were originally left open. This small window, or "Leper Squint", often cut diagonally through the wall near to the sanctuary meant that a sick person could stand outside the church and still see the altar. Its purpose was to give those who could not enter the church because they had leprosy the opportunity to participate at Mass. Another, less common, relic of those times is a device known as "Leper Tongs", special tweezers about a metre long used by the priest to give holy communion through the leper squint to those outside. Leper squints and tongs tell us two things about our mediaeval ancestors, the first being that they had compassion even on those who suffered from an illness they found horrific, wanting to give them whatever support and consolation they could, the second that leprosy in these islands was widespread at the time. It is a dreadful disease, and has truly been described as "a living death". It was no respecter of persons, it is known for a fact that Robert the Bruce, King of Scotland was a leper, and it is also more than possible that King Henry IV of England had the same disease. He certainly spent his last years isolated in the so-called "Jerusalem Chamber" of Westminster Abbey because he had a disfiguring skin disease. Recent forensic analysis of an 11th Century skull showed that its owner had suffered from leprosy, and of a kind carried by the red squirrel, and it is thought that the disease spread through trade in squirrel meat and fur. Thanks to modern medicine, the disease is now rare in this country.

Leprosy was very common in the Middle East at the time of Our Blessed Lord. The risk of infection was real. Many people in those days believed that illness came as a consequence of human sin and wickedness, with the nastiest diseases reserved for the worst sinners, and that these poor, pitiful and disfigured creatures were bad people suffering the anger of God. For reasons of both bodily and spiritual hygiene, lepers were to be avoided at all costs. If a family member showed signs of the disease, they would at once be thrown out of their home, disowned by their family. The "Kaddish"(the Jewish funeral prayers) would be read out, and from that time they would be accounted as dead people. The sufferer would be forbidden to approach any town or village, but must cover their head with a veil and shout "Unclean! Unclean!" If anyone came near.

I have often wondered what gave the poor leper in today's Gospel the courage even to approach Jesus. He ran the real risk of people hurling stones at him, hurting - maybe even killing him. Had he spoken to anyone, or was it just something in the way Our Lord looked at the sick man, standing apart from everyone else? Saint Mark doesn't tell us, so we have no way of knowing, but somehow or other, that leper found the courage to trust Jesus, and draw near to him.

The poor suffering man opened the conversation by telling Jesus that He could cure him if it was His will - God alone could cure a leper. This unfortunate man understood that his illness was in some incomprehensible way God's will for him. He recognised the power of God in Jesus, but he expressed his prayer in a beautiful way, everything conditional on the will of God. Later on, Jesus would teach his followers to pray "Thy will be done", words which He himself would speak to His Father as He sweated blood in Gethsemane.

Saint Mark tells us now what Jesus felt, what He did, and what he said:

Jesus felt compassion. His Sacred Heart burns with love and compassion for all humanity, and there are no exceptions. Just to experience that radiant, loving compassion must have overwhelmed the leper. Meditating on those three words: "Jesus felt compassion" has moved many a Christian to tears, maybe you are one of them. I certainly am.

Jesus reached out and touched the man. That would have been the first touch of a healthy, loving human hand he had felt for years. Sickness is not a sign of God's disfavour. Jesus does not find the man offensive or repulsive. He is not sickened by the stench of the diseased body, or the filthy rags covering it. The Divine Pity rises above all human hesitation. Imagine that - first the compassionate gaze, then the loving touch.

Jesus said "Be cured", and the man's leprosy "left him at once". He went his way excited and rejoicing. In his excitement, he forgot that Jesus had ordered him not to say anything till he had been to a priest, made the prescribed sacrifice, and been given a clean bill of health. As a result of this, many local people, afraid that Jesus might Himself have become infected by the disease, refused to let Him near them. When we live good lives, we can attract others to Jesus and His Church, but when we forget what He has taught, we can just as easily put them off.

Lent begins next Wednesday. It is a time of repentance. Have there been times when you and I were not a good advertisement for the Catholic Church? Do others feel the same compassionate love of Christ in our words and actions? Lent is a time to take a good hard look at our own selves - but not stay focused on our own failings, for it is above all a time to look towards Jesus, to feel His compassionate gaze and His loving touch in the Sacrament of Penance, and to hear those precious words: "Your sins are forgiven, go in peace."

****

1st Sunday of Lent   Repent and believe the Good News!

Gospel Reading: Mark 1:12-15

We have just heard what is by far and away the shortest Gospel account of Our Lord's temptation in the desert. Saint Matthew's occupies seventeen verses and Saint Luke's thirteen; Saint Mark, never one to waste words, uses just two verses! He doesn't give any detail of the temptations at all. He confines himself to just four points: the Spirit drove Jesus into the desert to fast and pray at length, there He was tempted by Satan, He was with the wild animals, and angels ministered to Him.

Mark then immediately moves to the beginning of Our Lord's preaching:

"The time is fulfilled, and the Kingdom of God has drawn near. Repent and believe in the Gospel!" (Mark 1:15}

Today, I ask you to join me in a short reflection on those words:

Repent, and believe in the Gospel (which means "Good News").

When we receive the blessed ashes at the beginning of Lent, those self-same words are often used - most appropriate to Lent, suggesting as they do two very helpful ways in which we can improve the quality of our lives in Christ. We are encouraged to do two things: turn away from sin and have faith in the Good News.

"Turn away from sin" is not so much about stopping something we have been doing, but rather about starting to do something better. Sin is often characterised in the Bible as "darkness". In his great Prologue (John 1), St. John describes the Word thus:

"The light shines in the darkness, and the darkness cannot comprehend it."

In our lives we are constantly called upon to choose between good and bad, virtue and vice, sin and holiness. Just before that great Catholic author and apologist G. K. Chesterton died, he spoke for one last time:

"The issue is clear - it is a battle between light and darkness, and each of us must choose his side."

Lent is a time to remind ourselves of that, and to ask: "Which way am I facing - am I looking towards the darkness or the light?". When we turn away from sin, there is only one other way we can be looking: towards God. Conversely, when we are no longer looking at God we must needs be facing the darkness. In life, things are either right or wrong, true or false, life-giving or life-destroying. We are always travelling in one direction or the other, heading either for light or darkness, life or death. No compromise is possible. Sadly, our fallen human nature rather hinders us here. A bird must work hard beating its wings in order to stay in the air; if that effort ceases, it simply falls to the ground under the influence of gravity. There is a law of gravity in the spiritual life too, unless we are making a conscious and deliberate effort to move towards the light, we will inevitably fall towards the darkness. Perhaps this is an opportune moment to recall the words of the Greek philosopher Socrates "There is no greater tragedy than an unexamined life" Saint Ignatius of Loyola prescribes a daily "Examen", an assessment of each day, our choices, attitudes, actions and reactions, to ask in which direction we have been tending hour by hour, day by day - "When I said or thought this or did that, was I making the effort to rise towards the light, or allowing myself to fall into the darkness?". We need to be very clear in this: The only way to turn away from sin is to face God.

Facing God can, in the first instance, be far from pleasant. This is why the spiritual life is not always the happy, ecstatic and care-free emotional experience we might like it to be. If a garden is overgrown, nobody notices during the night, but its shabbiness cannot be hidden in the light of day. The same is true in an untidy house, and of an untidy life too! As soon as we face the light, we become aware of the true state we are in. It is then that we need to remember the words "Have faith in the Good News" because all too often when we see the shabbiness of our lives we are tempted to despair.

The "Good News" at the heart of the teaching of Our Blessed Lord is that God is our loving Father, ever ready to welcome home the wandering child. Jesus describes himself as the Good Shepherd who will go to any length to rescue one single lost sheep, and rejoices to bring it home again.

Saint Paul expresses his own human weakness and his confidence in God's mercy when he says:

"Unhappy man that I am, who will free me from this body of death? The grace of God, by Jesus Christ our Lord!" (Romans 7:24)

And he goes on to tell us *"Do not allow evil to prevail, instead prevail over evil by means of goodness."* (Romans 12:21)

Yes, we need to be aware of our sins, but not to become obsessed with them. When once we have sought God's forgiveness for our sins they are forgiven for good and all. To brood upon them is to glance back into the darkness. The best advice for someone who is afraid of heights is "don't look down". There is an equally good piece of spiritual advice "when you're looking at God, don't keep turning round to look behind". Have faith in the Good News.

The weeks ahead are the time for our "Easter Duties". The

Church requires Catholics to receive Holy Communion during Eastertide, and to celebrate the Sacrament of Reconciliation if they are able to do so. There, with God's help we find the courage to confess any grave sins, and also speak of other problems, shortcomings and defects which may concern us. We can experience the healing ministry of Jesus at first hand, hearing His welcoming and healing words. We also receive sacramental grace which helps us to keep looking towards the light in the future.

May God give us all the grace this Lent to face the light, to deal with those things in ourselves which that light reveals and, trusting in His loving mercy to have the courage to confess our sins and be healed of them.

****

2nd Sunday of Lent   Seeking the face of Jesus

Gospel Reading: Mark 9:2-10

Our Bishop's motto is "Quaerite Christi Vultum" - "Seek the face of Christ".

Let me begin by asking you something: What does the Lord look like to you? What face is it you see when you pray? That's a complicated question, isn't it? We carry with us several images of Jesus: the Babe of Bethlehem, the gentle and compassionate Good Shepherd, the glorious and majestic face of Christ the King. These are consoling images. Others make us less comfortable: Christ as Judge, and above all Christ suffering. We may not like to think of the sufferings of Jesus, but if we look around the church, with its Crucifix and Stations of the Cross, we clearly see that the suffering face of Jesus stands at the very heart of our faith.

As we begin this second week of Lent, our Gospel offers us hope. The story itself, however, must be correctly understood in order that both Christian Faith and Hope may rest upon a safe and solid foundation. A wise theologian once said that holding on to the virtue of Hope is very hard as we grow older because our experience of life shows us that practically always, practically everything goes wrong. In fact, the only hope which will never disappoint us is a true Christian hope which is deeply rooted in the person of our Lord Jesus Christ.

To understand and gain most benefit from the Gospel today, we really need to approach the Transfiguration from three different angles:

1. When did it happen?
2. Where did it happen?
3. Why did it happen?

The Gospel says that the Transfiguration took place about a week after that eventful day at Caesarea Philippi. First of all Peter had proclaimed Jesus as Messiah, and the Son of the Living God, and been told by Jesus that he, Simon was are a blessed man. Immediately afterwards, Our Lord revealed to Peter and his companions that He must go to Jerusalem to suffer and die. This appalled them, Peter immediately told Jesus that this must not be allowed to happen, and was roundly rebuked with the words "Get behind me, Satan!". His closest followers, represented by Peter, had come to recognise and welcome the radiant face of Jesus as Lord and Christ, but they recoiled from the thought of that same face, battered, bruised, and contorted with pain.

Now we move to the "where?". It took place on a mountain, not actually named in the Bible, but traditionally identified as Tabor (though some scholars think Mount Hermon more likely). The geography isn't really that important. Jesus tended to go up hills when He wanted to be alone with His Father in prayer. In taking His disciples up a mountain, He was telling them (and us too) that we can never even begin to understand the meaning of the cross without a good deal of prayer. He took them away from their familiar surroundings, occupations and distractions to help them focus on Himself alone. Lent calls us to try to distance ourselves from as much distraction as we can, so as to pray better. Mountain climbing is hard work, and prayer is often an uphill struggle too. The mountain is important.

Now the "why?" Let us turn to Thomas Aquinas who said:

"Our Lord, after foretelling His Passion to His disciples, had exhorted them to follow the path of His sufferings. Now in order that anyone go straight along a road, he must have some knowledge of the end: thus an archer will not shoot the arrow straight unless he first see the target." (Summa Theol. III.45).

The great English scholar Saint Bede the Venerable wrote:

"By his loving foresight he allowed them to taste for a short time the contemplation of eternal joy so that they might bear persecution bravely". (Commentary on St. Matthew)

More recently, Pope Francis said:

"The event of the Transfiguration of Our Lord offers us a

message of hope; it invites us to encounter Jesus, and to be of service to our brothers." (Pope Francis, Angelus Message, 6 August 2017)

Let's think again of our own problems with the suffering face of Christ. The Catholic Faith and the experience of life both teach us that it is the most frequent face of Jesus we see in our lives, reflected in His suffering brothers and sisters the world over, and inevitably in our own face at times when we look in a mirror. It is so very hard to understand or to accept. The very existence of suffering in the world is the reason many people give for not believing in God at all. Even for believers, it is a mystery too deep to comprehend: "Tis mystery all," wrote Charles Wesley, "the Immortal dies, who can unfold His deep design?"

Contemplating the Transfiguration, we see Our Blessed Lord with his chosen friends. Many people at the time came to Jesus to see the face of the dynamic Rabbi, the Healer, the Wonder Worker, but these are only part of the story. Jesus Christ is far more than the sum of his words and actions. One of the greatest obstacles to a deep prayer life is the desire forever to be doing, making and getting. We become so obsessed with doing that we neglect just being. The reality of who we are is much more than the things we do. On that mountain top, Peter, James and John saw for an instant into the depths of their Master's being. St. Peter would later recall this in his Second Epistle:

*"For he received honour and glory from God the Father,
whose voice descended to him from the magnificent glory:
"This is my beloved Son, in whom I am well pleased. Listen to
him." We also heard this voice conveyed from heaven, when
we were with him on the holy mountain..." (2 Peter 1:17-18)*

Years later, Peter remembered that moment when he was "knocked sideways" with that intimate knowledge of Jesus. He had seen the face of God, and been forever changed.

The Gospel today tells us a very basic spiritual truth. Our faith is about coming to know a person: faith is a personal invitation into an intimate friendship with Jesus. Yes, we need to have structures, organisation, authority, doctrine, formal worship, learned prayers, but these things are all road signs, warning notices, sometimes "grab rails". In the end we must yield our innermost selves to Jesus, and allow Him time, space and silence to speak to our own hearts.

That is how we too can come to be stunned by a glimpse of His glorious face, and eternally changed by it.

****

3rd Sunday of Lent   Hearing and Understanding

Gospel reading: John 2:13-25

A priest I once knew had a plaque on his study wall which read:

"I know you think you understand what you believe you heard me say, but I'm not sure you realise that what you heard is not what I meant!"

A simple lack of communication lies at the heart of the majority of our problems with other people. Most of a Spiritual Counsellor's work consists of listening to what other people say, and then making sure he or she understands what is actually being said. This is often done by telling the other person what you have heard, and so often evoking the response: "No, you've misunderstood me, that isn't what I meant!" Coming to understand what people are actually saying to you can be a long, demanding process, calling for much tact and patience. In the same way, Relationship Counsellors spend much of their time trying to help people to listen to one another, and thus come to mutual understanding. Truth to tell, it can be just as hard to understand our own selves, our feelings, desires, motives and actions, as it is to understand another person. We human beings struggle to say what we mean, mean what we say, and understand what others say to us. Technology has given us printing, telephones, radio, TV and the Internet, and we have far better and faster communications than ever before. Ironically, just like the Tower of Babel in the Bible, this has simply increased the speed with which we can misunderstand others, and spread our misconceptions all over the world!

If understanding other people is so very hard, however can we hope to understand God? We are well accustomed to describing prayer as "Conversing with God" (NOT "Talking to God", please!). Any real conversation has to include both listening and speaking. When we are taught to pray, we learn things to say to God, but listening and understanding? That's a horse of a different colour! We have learned that the Bible is the Word of God, but as we have already seen, hearing the words does not automatically mean we have understood them. Indeed, the Holy Bible is packed full of stories about people who, having heard the words, failed to grasp the meaning. Last Sunday, for instance, our first reading told the story of the sacrifice of Abraham, our father in Faith. He was just about to kill his own son when God brought him to understand that, unlike pagan gods, the One True God does not demand human sacrifice.

Today's Gospel also says much about hearing God's word but missing the meaning. In the story there are three distinct parts:

1. Jesus throws the traders out of the Temple,

2. He promises to "rebuild the Sanctuary in three days".

3. Saint John tells us that Jesus "knew what was in a man's heart".

Our first reading today was a long account of God giving His Law to the Jewish people. His requirements seem quite clear, yet those who received the Law struggled from age to age in understanding and keeping it. Even while Moses was up on Mount Sinai being told:

"You shall not make yourselves a graven image or any likeness.... you shall not adore them, nor shall you worship them" (Exodus 20:4)

The people down the mountain were busy making themselves a golden idol to worship!

In the same way, the traders and money-changers in the Jerusalem Temple had heard God say through His prophet Isaiah:

"My house will be called a house of prayer" (56:7)

but they had still turned it into a market where, not God's prophet, but the "god of profit" was their guiding star. Sadly, many still hitch their wagon to that deceptive star!

When Our Blessed Lord interrupted their operations, it was not just the traders who were upset, the worshippers were also outraged. They too had heard the word but missed the meaning. "Give us a sign" they demanded "to justify what you have done."

2. The reply they received was both unexpected and mysterious. "Destroy this Sanctuary, and in three days I will raise it up". Predictably enough, those who heard failed to understand that Jesus was speaking of His own Resurrection, not some record-breaking building project. Saint John tells us that not even the Disciples themselves grasped the meaning of those words till they had witnessed Our Lord's Resurrection.

All we have heard so far demonstrates our human tendency not to listen carefully when God is speaking. Understanding only comes with silence and time, neither of which feature nearly enough in our liturgy or our personal prayer lives. Lent is a call to become attentive listeners to God.

3. We struggle to understand God, but how well does God understand us? Here at least is good news, God perfectly understands each and every human person. We can't fool God or try to conceal parts of our lives with "smoke and mirrors". There is an ancient Islamic prayer, attributed to Abu Bakr, Mohammed's father-in-law, which begins: "O God, I thank thee, for thou knowest me better than I know

myself". It's reassuring that God understands us, even when we don't understand ourselves. We may well struggle to find words when we pray, but the words are of little importance. What matters is that we consciously place ourselves in God's presence, knowing ourselves to be fully understood and loved beyond all understanding. *"Be still and know that I am God"* *(Psalm 46:11)* – these words are the best ever instruction manual for prayer. Presence, silence, listening - such is the essence of all true prayer. "Words are all we have" said the writer Samuel Becket. Luckily, he was quite wrong. Words are nothing without meaning, hearing is useless without understanding.

When Pope Saint John Paul II visited Britain in 1982, I myself was privileged to hear his opening words: "People of Britain, I have come to call you to Jesus, to call you to prayer." During this third week of Lent, can we all try to respond to that call in silent and attentive prayer?

****

4th Sunday of Lent   Light and darkness

Gospel Reading: John 3:14-21

Nicodemus, we are told "went to Jesus by night" (John 3:1). This has at times led to people saying and writing silly things about him. The severe Protestant autocrat John Calvin coined the word "Nicodemite", which he applied to anyone he felt was not fully committed in their Christian belief and behaviour. He even wrote a whole book, condemning the "Nicodemites" to eternal punishment no different from the unbeliever and the heathen. ("Excuse de Jehan Calvin, a Messieurs des Nicodemites", 1544) I have heard preachers say that Nicodemus "only believed half-heartedly and came to Jesus at night because he was afraid of being seen with Our Lord, and being thought the less of." This judgement ignores other things the Gospel tells us about this worthy man. He appears three times in the New Testament, once when he came to see Jesus at night, then when he spoke out boldly in the Great Council, insisting that Jesus must be given a fair and proper hearing, despite the hostility of the others (John 7:50). Lastly, we are told that he gave precious embalming spices and helped Joseph of Arimathea to bury the dead body of Jesus. (John 19:39), neither of those two actions show a man afraid of being associated with Jesus, do they?

What sort of man was Nicodemus then? He was a Pharisee

and a member of the Sanhedrin, the ruling council of the Jews. Unusually, for a Pharisee, he had a Greek name, formed of two words "Nike" meaning "Victory" and "Demos" - "of the people". It is thought that he came from a family well-known as negotiators and peace-makers (cf. Barclay "The Gospel of John" Vol 1 p. 123). Again, for a Pharisee he was a very open-minded man. The Pharisees believed that the best time to contemplate and discuss the Law of God was by night, which may in itself explain his late visit. Alternatively, it could simply be that the only time he could get anywhere near Jesus and have a private conversation was at night. The meeting Saint John records was a warm and cordial one. Nicodemus, the peace-maker, struck up a deep and lasting friendship with the young Rabbi who had said *"Blessed are the peace-makers, for they shall be called sons of God" (Matthew 5:9).* Think kindly of Nicodemus, he deserves it.

We heard just one part of their long conversation this morning. The words of Jesus revolve around the twin themes of darkness and light. At the very beginning of his Gospel, Saint John describes the Incarnate Word of God as a light the darkness could not overcome (cf. John 1:5) Early in Saint Luke's Gospel, we hear old Simeon describing the newborn Son of God as a Light to enlighten the gentiles, the glory of His people Israel (cf. Luke 2:21).

The theme of darkness recurs throughout the Bible, and

always portends evil or confusion. We will hear this in our Easter Vigil Mass. It was out of the chaos and darkness of a formless void that God began the work of creation by commanding *"Let there be light!"* (Genesis 1:1-3). Pharaoh refused to let the Children of Israel go free, so Egypt was punished with ten plagues, the ninth being darkness covering the whole land (Exodus 10:21). Isaiah the prophet promised the Messiah as a "Great Light" to shine on a people that "walked in darkness" (cf. Isaiah 9:2). In the Gospels, we hear of Jesus curing the blind (Mark 10:46) and condemning his critics for their inner blindness (Matthew 15:14) When Judas leaves the Last Supper to betray Jesus for his paltry purse of silver, Saint John ominously tells us "It was night" (13:31). At the crucifixion darkness covered the whole land from the sixth to the ninth hour (cf. Luke 23:44) On Easter morning, the empty tomb was discovered at sunrise, the break of day (Luke 24:1)

There are many, many more instances. Altogether, in the Bible, the theme of darkness occurs nearly 200 times. Encouragingly, that of light can be found on more than 300 occasions! There will always be more light than darkness, God's grace exceeds our emptiness, God's forgiveness is infinitely greater than our capacity to sin.

"For God so loved the world that He gave His only Son, that

whoever believes in Him should not perish but have eternal life" (John 3:16)

The Pharisees saw God as a "Jealous God" who took careful note of every human transgression, however small, and then punished the sins of the fathers in the sons and the grandsons, to the third and fourth generation (cf. Exodus 34:7). Imagine the impact of the words of Jesus on Nicodemus, the lover of peace. I once heard a man describe the moment he embraced God's gift of faith. He said "It was as though a light went on inside my head." Surely Nicodemus felt the same, he had longed for peace and heard that God was not hostile towards humanity, but was prepared to go to any lengths to bring us safely to everlasting life.

The philosopher Leibnitz was once asked what question he would most like answered. He replied "I would ask: 'Is the universe a friendly place?'." Nicodemus now knew the answer, and that knowledge of God's infinite love, drawing us to everlasting life, must surely be the very heart of the Good News of Our Lord Jesus Christ. Saint Paul wrote to the early Christians in Corinth, telling that Christ's love overwhelms us when we reflect that He died for us all, so that our new life in Christ should be lived, not for our own selves, but for the One who died and was rose to life for us (cf .2 Corinthians 5:14). Jesus said: *"I came that they may have life and have it more abundantly"* (John 10:10)

Nicodemus, good man though he might be, was truly "in the dark" and the greater part of it was that he was so desperately afraid of a demanding and angry God. In that darkness, he had the good sense to come to Jesus and hear words of mercy, love and life. In this Fourth Week of Lent, we too are called to rejoice that we have heard those same words. In darkness and doubt, Jesus calls us to himself, that we may gaze upon Him, lifted up from the earth, and receive His promise of salvation.

An American priest once found himself sharing a train journey with a well-known comedian. Predictably enough, the comic wanted to get a laugh out of his companion.

"I suppose," he said in a loud voice "you're going to try and sell me some of your Fire Insurance!" There was instant laughter, and the priest joined in, but when the laughter died down, he smiled at the comedian and replied:

"No, my friend, not "Fire Insurance" but LIFE ASSURANCE!"

****

5th Sunday of Lent   Living with Mystery

Being a Lincolnshire man, born and bred, I feel great affection for my native County's famous sons and daughters, not least the great physicist Sir Isaac Newton. His body is buried in Westminster Abbey, graced with an epitaph written by the poet Alexander Pope:

"Nature and Nature's laws lay hid in night: God said: "Let Newton be, and all was light!"

Present Day physicists are wise not to claim their ability to "make all things light". A prudent man of science acknowledged the truth that there is more to the universe than any human mind is capable of understanding or describing. They identify what some physicists describe as paradoxes, anomalies and inconsistencies which defy the Laws of Physics as we know them. Some have gone on to say that the things which don't behave the way scientists think that they should are "mistakes" and "imperfections".

Believers, of course, would give another name to that which is beyond all scientific investigation and definition - and that is GOD.

To describe things we can't understand as mistakes and inconsistencies can never be good enough for someone with faith. Three hundred years ago, people believed that Isaac

Newton had answered all the questions about the way the universe worked. Later scientists, notably Einstein, showed that even the great Newton had made his mistakes. What of the scientists today, can they really hope to answer all the questions? Could it not be that, where there find anomalies and inconsistencies, the mistake is in their own theories and calculations? Might it not be that there is an intelligence infinitely greater than theirs behind creation? When you come to think about it, is it any easier to believe that everything started in a huge, chaotic explosion of matter than it is to believe in an intelligent Creator of heaven and earth?

Think about a great work of art such as the Mona Lisa or the ceiling of the Sistine Chapel. Would it make sense to suggest that either one had come about as the result of an explosion in a paint factory? Surely it **would** make more sense to recognise and appreciate the skill of the gifted artist who applied paint with such skill.

Then again, who could look at a magnificent piece of engineering like a space rocket or a massive suspension bridge, and suggest that it was merely the result of a freak whirlwind hitting a scrap yard?

Truth to tell, nobody believes in nothing. Some people who would describe themselves as "non-believers" have faith in science or political philosophy. They are the sensible ones, others believe in ley lines, crystals, fairies, dragons and lucky charms. As G. K. Chesterton is said to have remarked: "When men choose not to believe in God, they do not thereafter believe in nothing, they then become capable of believing in anything!"

This much is sure, science, politics and philosophy have changed many times in the last two thousand years, and they go on changing. The Good News alone is unchanged and unchanging. *"Jesus Christ is the same yesterday, today, and for ever." (Hebrews 13:8)*

We have seen in recent weeks that Our Lord's teaching was, in its own time, often seen to be inconsistent with what others wanted to believe. He said much that was paradoxical. As I've remarked before, in the end, He could only be judged to be mad, bad or God, no other conclusion was, or is, possible. For Jewish people in those days, what they termed the "Son of Man" (Bar Nasha) was a superhuman, all-conquering hero whose glorification would be conclusive victory over the armies of all "The Nations", and rule over all the world as an absolute monarch. Jesus, however, while describing Himself as Son of Man spoke of a very different glorification which involved rejection, condemnation, crucifixion, death and failure. He would be lifted up to be sure, but His throne would be a rough wooden cross on top of a rubbish tip, and His crown would be made of thorns. Like a grain of wheat, He must die and be buried in the ground in order to rise again.

It took a lot of faith for even his closest friends to accept this. Saint Peter himself struggled with the very idea. At the Transfiguration, Peter, James and John had glimpsed His divinity for one blinding and glorious instant, but now back down the mountain, they had to cope with a very different reality. There had to be death before resurrection, the cross before kingship. Each of them faced the same inevitable question: who is wrong, Jesus or me? One or the other had to be mistaken. This is the ultimate "acid test" of faith, and none of us escapes it. Like poor old Job, in the end we must either reject God, or put our finger to our lips and stand silent in the presence of mystery.

A theology professor, under whom I studied many moons ago, used to say that an appropriate "signature tune" for God would be the song "I was born under a Wandering Star" because He is like the horizon - you reach that distant point only to find another horizon. God is like an ever-flowing spring: however many times we satisfy our thirst, we can never drink it all. The Prophet Isaiah (Chapter 58:11) speaks of God giving us *"A fountain of water, whose waters will not fail."* People have sometimes asked me "Won't eternity be boring?"- I don't believe it will, you know. If there are always new horizons presented by God's love which is "new every morning", then we will be caught up in the greatest of adventures, as Cardinal

Newman wrote "hearing no longer the busy beat of time" ("The Dream of Gerontius" 1865, part 2) .

The readings in recent weeks have been very much about living with questions, embracing mystery, going by faith and not by sight. To be silent before God, to accept that there are mysteries far beyond our understanding, to live with the questions we can't answer - these are the non-negotiable "Terms and Conditions" of Christian Faith.

And what of the non-believers? In Eucharistic Prayer IV, we pray for all those who seek God "in sincerity of heart". In seeking the Truth, unknowingly people seek Him, for God is Truth. In the General Intercessions on Good Friday afternoon the Church prays that those who do not acknowledge God may sincerely follow what is right, thus finding the way to God Himself. I don't think we should limit our prayers for that intention to one day every year, do you?

****

Palm Sunday   Were you there?

Gospel reading: Mark 15:1-39

The beautiful hymn "My Song is Love Unknown" is often sung in Holy Week. It asks a searching question: "Ah, who am I that for my sake my Lord should take frail flesh and die?"......Who am I? We are told that the daily prayer of St. Francis of Assisi was: "My God, who are you - and who am I?". Lent is meant to be a "Grounding Experience" in our spiritual lives, paradoxically bringing us down to earth so that we might the better seek heaven! The bedrock of true spirituality is in that twin question: Who is God? Who am I?

There's an old Negro Spiritual that asks: "Were you there when they crucified my Lord?"

Listening to the Passion of Our Lord this morning, and then asking ourselves that question can give a more unvarnished answer to that "Who am I?" because, truth to tell we were all there. Every human emotion is played out in the Passion story, all the psychological complexity of humanity, capable of such goodness, and such badness.

So where do you find yourself in the story? There are plenty of places to look:

Maybe a face in the crowd overcome with enthusiasm, waving

their palms, cheering the celebrity, unsure just who He is; easily moved by public opinion so that Sunday's "Hosannas" can become Friday's "Crucify him!".

Then there's Simon Peter who seems to be Jesus' best friend, but struggles to understand Our Lord. Peter speaks brave words, can react with sudden violence in defence of his Master, yet in the courtyard will deny Him to save his own skin.

What about Pontius Pilate, the authority figure who is torn between his desire to please his Emperor and the Jerusalem Mob, and at the same time the knowledge that Jesus is an innocent man. Pilate the cynic, the worldly-wise man who doesn't believe there is such a thing as truth, literally "washes his hands" of the business, yet is personally responsible for a hideous miscarriage of justice.

The women of Jerusalem weep to witness the mindless cruelty of the execution. They know there's nothing they can do to alter things, and truly weep "for themselves and their children", the helpless victims of life's tragedies who can still find it in their hearts to weep and pray for another suffering human being.

Two thieves also die that day. One vents his spleen, cursing and reviling Jesus for failing to provide him with an escape route; somehow he typifies many who want God only to solve their problems and take away their pain, and angrily reject God when He doesn't oblige. The other recognises his own utter emptiness of anything but guilt and just condemnation. He turns to the innocent One, asking only "Jesus, remember me".

What of Our Mother Mary, stunned and silent at the foot of the Cross, her heart pierced through with sorrow's sharp sword? How could her soul "glorify the Lord" for what she now witnessed? What did it mean to rejoice in God her Saviour as her beloved Son died so terribly? Maybe for you too that God who once seemed so close, whose touch brought such joy, now seems as remote as a far-distant Galaxy.

Simon of Cyrene helps in spite of himself. He'd far rather not get involved, he feels no enthusiasm for his task and perhaps little satisfaction afterwards, and yet he helps Jesus with the weight of his cross. Joseph of Aramthea and Nicodemus have a lot to lose in associating themselves with Jesus, far more than many others who have turned, looked away, run away. People of principle and conviction, they will stand their ground in the face of an opposing tide of public opinion. In the perennial struggle between good and evil, every just cause will be theirs too.

Were you there? Oh yes, without doubt you were, just as I

was. So who are you in the story? It's a hard question because one can so easily find elements of one's own character, good and bad, in so many of the cast.

This Holy Week is not just a commemoration of an historical event, Much more than that, it is a call to discover our true selves with and in Jesus.

Who is God........who am I?

"And can it be that I should gain
An int'rest in the Saviour's blood?
Died He for me, who caused His pain?
For me, who Him to death pursued?
Amazing love! how can it be
That Thou, my God, shouldst die for me?

(Charles Wesley)

****

Holy Thursday Do you understand what I have done?

Gospel reading: John 13:1-15

The traditional English title for today is "Maundy Thursday". It is derived from the Latin "Mandatum", meaning "Commandment". This was the day when Jesus gave a very special commandment to us, His followers. The commandment is twofold, and we celebrate both parts, not just in this Mass, but at each and every Mass. Both halves of the "Mandatum" are themselves given in two parts: first Jesus shows us what he wants us to do, then he commands us to do the same.

The Gospels situate the whole "Mandatum" within the Last Supper, the great Passover Meal which Jesus shared with His disciples the night before He died to save the whole world. As Jews, the disciples were very familiar with the Passover Feast. The family meal, remembering the Lord God's deliverance of his people from slavery in Egypt, would have been at the heart of their faith from their earliest days. Eating the lamb reminded them of the lamb's blood which had marked out the Jewish homes in Egypt so that the Angel of Death "passed over" their homes. The blood kept them safe when all around them the firstborn child of every family, from greatest to least, was taken by death. The lamb was accompanied by bitter herbs, a reminder of the bitterness of slavery and captivity, and by unleavened bread, recalling their hasty departure from Egypt.

Wine brought to mind the blessedness and joy of God's people.

At this Passover Meal, however, there were two important changes. When Jesus, as host of the meal, took bread and broke it, He did not merely recall the Exodus of old, and neither did the cup of wine He blessed simply symbolise the joy of God's blessings. No, He said "Take, eat - this is my Body which will be given up for you ; Take, drink - this is my Blood which will be shed for you.". Then He gave His "Mandatum": "Do this in memory of me". The annual sacrificial lamb is now superseded by the eternal sacrifice of the Lamb of God. Although offered "once, only once, and once for all", this self-same sacrifice is nevertheless available in our own time through the Holy Mass. The Eucharist is not just a "remembering", for when we do this in His memory, that same Sacred Body, given up for us, and Precious Blood, shed for us, becomes really and truly present, Body, Blood Soul and Divinity, and we are called, though unworthy, to welcome Him "under our roof".

At the Last Supper, Jesus celebrated the first Mass, but more was to come. The meal ended, He proceeded to wash the feet of the disciples. This astounded them! The washing of feet was seen as the most menial and degrading of tasks in those days. Jewish Rabbinic teaching required a Rabbi's disciples to be his servants in all respect but one - they must not be asked to wash their master's feet. This job was for the lowest of the low among the household and was, wherever possible, done by a slave. Yet now their Master washed their feet. Not for the first time, Simon Peter failed to understand or accept what was happening, and told Jesus "No, you'll never wash my feet!" Jesus answered him by saying that he must accept this humble action or "have no part in Him", and Peter yielded to His will. Then the Lord asked them all whether they understood what He had done for them; they needed to understand that God, their Lord and Master, had come among them as a servant. God came to earth, not to look down on us in lofty judgement. He came not to tread us underfoot from above, but to lift us up from beneath.

Do we understand this? Much is said these days of the need of a "New Evangelisation", but in truth there cannot be one. Jesus Christ is the same yesterday, today and tomorrow, and the Good News of Jesus Christ is unchanged by the changing years. No "new" preaching of the Gospel is needed. Perhaps, however, it needs to be proclaimed with greater understanding. Saint Paul tells us "I live, yet now it is not I, but truly Christ who lives in me" (Galatians 2:20). Accepting that, we must also accept the fact that living with Christ demands that we too should live as Christ, the humble, self-sacrificing Servant. A Christian community which truly understands this will work hard to leave behind self-importance, self-aggrandisement, pride, ambition and the cult of personality, seeking just like Jesus to lift our poor world up from below. Such a community will not needs schemes and programmes of evangelisation and Catechesis, by God's grace they will happen of their own accord. Christianity, it has been said, cannot be "taught", it can only be "caught."

In our Mass this Holy Thursday evening, our prayer is that the Lord will help us better to hear and understand His "Mandatum", so that we may spread His infectious Love far and wide.

****

Easter Sunday   The stone and the empty tomb

Gospel reading: Mark 16:1-8

It is fashionable these days for people to tell us that Easter is no more than the "Christianisation" of an old Nordic Feast in honour of a fertility goddess known as "Ostra". As the song goes, however "This ain't necessarily so"! In the first place, Christianity began in the Middle East, and didn't reach this part of the world until the second century, when (let us remember) the population were Celts and Romano-British, neither of whom spoke Anglo-Saxon. Most other languages derive their name for Easter from the Jewish "Pasch", for Jesus died and rose during the Passover Festival. In Roman Britain the Christians did the same, and we do still use the word "Paschal" in English today. The Nordic Fertility Goddess was not called "Ostra", but "Freya" (from which "Friday" is derived). The earliest reference to "Ostra" is to be found in the Venerable Bede's Ecclesiastical History of the 8th Century AD. There, he refers to the Anglo Saxon "Ostra-monad", which many since have chosen to translate as "Ostra's Month". In fact, the Anglo-Saxon word "Ost" simply means "East", and they called the month of April "Oster-end" meaning "East wind". It remains the case that the prevailing wind in England at this time of the year is an Easterly one - and I keep a daily record of the weather.

Goddess "Ostra"? - not a bit of it! Just as the practical Anglo-

Saxons called the run up to Easter "Lencten" (longer days), so they called the already centuries-old Christian Pasch "Oster-end" because that was the month it was celebrated.

So much for myths, now down to the truth. If you want to find uniquely Christian images for Easter, the place to look is in the Gospel. There we find two very powerful images: the heavy stone rolled back and the empty grave.

Think for a moment, and picture those holy women on their way to the tomb of Jesus. They are going as soon as they possibly can so as to complete the sketchy burial rituals of Good Friday. As soon as they can see at all, they hurry in the half-light towards the tomb, motivated by love alone. They are courageous: the tomb is guarded by soldiers, and they are walking into potential danger from those rough men in a secluded place, with no one to protect them. They are women of hope too. The tomb is sealed with a heavy stone. It would need several strong men to move that stone, so they can't be sure that they will be able to gain entry at all. In spite of all these concerns, those brave women continue their journey. When they arrive, they are amazed to find the soldiers gone, and the stone rolled back. There is no body in the tomb. Their first thought is not "Oh, Jesus has risen from the dead!" but "Someone has stolen the body!" - and wouldn't any of us react in the same way? They are set right by an angel who asks: "Why look among the dead for One who is alive? He is not here, He is risen!". They hurry back to share this news with Peter and the others, again (and justifiably) unsure of the reception their news will be given.

That journey to the tomb is, in many ways, reflected in our own experience of life. All human beings find their path through life a stony one; there are always little stones, the discomforts, niggles and problems relating to others - not to mention our own selves! At times, however, there are much bigger stones, and there seem to be obstacles we cannot either move or avoid looming ahead. Life is full of uncertainties, big worries and potential dangers to ourselves and those we love. These days, it is both fashionable and tempting to settle for "being a victim", unable or unwilling to move on, with only sympathy and self-pity to sustain us.

Then, of course, there is that huge and fearful stone awaiting us all - the gravestone! The fear of death, the reality of bereavement are constant, though unwelcome, companions on our journey through life, the more so the older we get. There was a saying very popular among my generation in the "Swinging Sixties" which I am quoting, albeit slightly edited: "Life is unpleasant, and then you die!"

Such is, of course, the only prospect facing a life lived without faith and hope in God. Christianity offers a very different narrative: the stones, even the very big ones, are often imaginary fears. The American President James Garfield famously remarked: "I am an old man and In my life I have known a great a great many troubles, but most of them never happened!". Even when the stones are very real, God always shows us a way round them, or sends welcome friends to help shift them.

The very best part of the Good News, however, is that the grave itself is unoccupied. The greatest of life's threats is no more than an empty one to a person with faith. The risen Jesus can be hard to find and recognise in our lives. This is because we so often look for Him in the wrong places. He is not among the dead, for He is alive. When those we love leave this world - when we ourselves do so, if we have made that uncertain journey of faith in the half light, we are not "among the dead" either, but alive in Christ!

The stone is moved, the grave stands empty. This is the heart of the Christian message. Eastern Catholics greet one another by saying "Christos Anesti!" (Christ is Risen!), which is answered "Alithos Anesti!" (He is Risen indeed!). Open your heart to those words today, welcome them, devour them, be nourished by them, cling to them in life and death.

Christ is Risen ... He is Risen indeed! Alleluia!

****

Second Sunday of Easter   *Divine Mercy*

Gospel reading: John 20:19-31

The Sunday after Easter is traditionally known as "Low Sunday". This strange name came about because the excitement of the Holy Week and Easter Ceremonies were now at an end, and the liturgy returned to a more usual pattern. In more recent years it has also become known as "Divine Mercy Sunday", so the choice is yours.

The Gospel for our Mass today is anything but "low key", however. We are told of Jesus appearing to his apostles, Thomas alone being absent. A week later, Jesus appeared to them again, and this time Thomas was there. These were undeniably "Peak Experiences" for the disciples, and filled them with faith, joy and excitement. This is in no way an anti-climax - on the contrary, it is about the disciples of Jesus experiencing a great growth in faith.

So there's no question of Low Sunday being "low key" when it comes to the Gospel. What of the "Divine Mercy" aspect then? There can be no denying that St. John's account of the two appearances of Jesus are filled with the mercy of Jesus Christ.

It would be a mistake if we came away from Mass this morning remembering only "Doubting Thomas". Most of the disciples simply ran away when Jesus was arrested in Gethsemane. Even St. Peter denied Jesus three times, and it seems to have been left to Joseph of Arimathea to arrange for the burial of Our Lord's body that first Good Friday. The evening of the first Easter Day found the disciples hiding away behind closed doors "for fear of the Jews", so it wasn't just Thomas who had problems with his faith - truth to tell, Peter and his companions were all in the same boat, and had little to be proud of.

It was to this band of frightened people, who had been tried and found wanting, that Jesus came. His first words must have astounded them: "Peace be with you" - of all the greetings from their abandoned and betrayed Master, none could have been more unexpected! No "What sort of friends are you then?", no "Where were you when I needed you?", simply "Peace be with you". The past is forgotten. Jesus shows them His wounded hands and side, reminding them that those wounds heal all our injuries, and that His precious blood washes all sin away.

Then Jesus tells them that they too must become instruments of reconciliation, bringing that Easter Peace to the world, with the power to forgive sin in His name.

Where was Thomas when all of this was going on? I have my own theory - read the Gospels carefully and you will see that

Thomas shows great courage. When the other disciples hesitated to follow Jesus to Jerusalem, it was Thomas who said *"Let us go too, that we may die with him".* *(John 11:16).* Perhaps he was the only one who dared go out into the hostile streets of Jerusalem to buy food or find water for the others. If so, what a disappointment for Thomas to find that his brave action had resulted in him missing the great event! Thomas wanted that same experience. He too wanted to see those wounds on the body of Jesus. He didn't ask for anything more than the others had already been given. Note though that his desire to see the Risen Lord was not immediately satisfied. He has to wait another week for his own meeting with Jesus. God answers every prayer and fulfils every hope, but in His own good time, not ours.

When Jesus comes for the second time, His greeting is the same "Peace be with you". There are no harsh words for the doubter, just an invitation to "Doubt no longer but believe", and Thomas does just that - "My Lord and my God".

There is a lovely hymn, seldom used in the Catholic Church, called "And Can It Be?". In it, Charles Wesley explores our own personal experience of Redemption in Jesus Christ. The second verse goes as follows:

"Tis mystery all, the Immortal dies, who can explore His strange design?

In vain, the firstborn Seraph tries to sound the depths of love divine.

Tis mercy all! Let earth adore, let Angel minds enquire no more".

Today's Mass is assuredly all about Divine Mercy. It is a great encouragement when doubts trouble us, the past disturbs us, or we are haunted by our own flawed discipleship. Psalm 85:9 reads: *"I will hear what the Lord God speaks, He speaks of peace for His people, and His faithful, and those who turn their heats to Him."* In prayer we too may hear those words. His wounded body speaks of a love which overcomes the darkness in our lives. "Tis mystery all" indeed, but none the less true for that. The heart of Jesus, wounded by our sins, still beats with love and mercy. The mystery of that love defies even the intellect of angels, who cannot "sound the depths of love divine", but the "Fount of love and mercy" will never run dry. Let us give St. Augustine the last word, and be encouraged in our prayer today:

"For in it is the fountain of life, which we must now thirst for in prayer so long as we live in hope, not yet seeing that which we hope for, trusting under the shadow of His wings before whom are all our desires, that we may be abundantly satisfied .... and made to drink of the river of His pleasures; because with Him is the fountain of life, and in His light we shall see light, when our desire shall be satisfied with good things, and when there shall be nothing beyond to be sought after with groaning, but all things shall be possessed by us with rejoicing." (Letter 130)

****

3rd Sunday of Easter *Witnesses to the Resurrection*

Gospel reading: Luke 24:35-48

The over-arching theme of this Sunday's Gospel is WITNESS.

Pope Saint Paul VI, speaking of the proclamation of the Gospel in our own time, wrote: "Modern man listens more willingly to witnesses than to teachers, and if he does listen to teachers, it is because they are witnesses." (Evangelii Nuntiandi, 1975, no. 41).

We heard of the Risen Jesus joining his friends in the Upper Room. In writing this passage Saint Luke himself bears witness to two fundamental Christian truths.

1. The necessity of the Cross. It would be true to say that all of the Old Testament looked forward towards the Cross, as Jesus himself taught his two disciples on the Emmaus Road. *"Was it not necessary the Christ should suffer these things and enter into His glory?". (Luke 24:26)* The crucifixion of Jesus of Nazareth did not happen just because the plan had "gone horribly wrong". It was always central to God's plan. During Lent we sing Isaac Watts' hymn "When I survey the wond'rous Cross", which asks "Did e'er such love and sorrow meet?". It was on Calvary that God's eternal love was shown in the most practical of ways through Jesus Christ, His only Son.

2. The reality of the Resurrection. At first, the disciples were terrified by the Lord's sudden appearance among them. They thought they were seeing a ghost; He asked why they were so agitated, and such doubts arose in their hearts.

Jesus invited them to voice their fears. It would seem, however, that they were reduced to terrified silence, so He went on to reassure them by showing His hands and feet, reassuring them that it was Himself indeed, inviting them to touch Him and see for themselves, for no ghost had flesh and bones.

The joy they now felt was still tinged with a sense of disbelief. It all seemed too good to be true. We are wisely warned to avoid tempting offers of "get rich quick" schemes by the sound advice that "If a thing seems too good to be true, it probably is!", so they still stood dumbfounded. Isn't it lovely to see Our Lord's patience in the face of their slowness to believe? He asks if they have anything to eat. They proffer a piece of grilled fish, which He proceeds to eat before their very eyes - a good-humoured and very practical demonstration that He is no phantom. The Christ who rose from the dead, and the Jesus who died on the cross are one and the same. Christianity is not the product of a fevered and disordered human imagination, but is founded on a real historical person who faced death, defeated death itself and rose again.

"And," said Jesus *"for so it is written, and so it was necessary for the Christ to suffer and to rise up from the dead on the third day, and in his name, for repentance and the forgiveness of sins to be preached among all the nations ."(Luke 24:6-77)*

Both of those great truths are proclaimed to us, and by us, each time we celebrate the Eucharist. We proclaim the mystery of faith: "Lord, by Your cross and resurrection you have set us free. You are the Saviour of the World!"

Each successive generation of Christian people is called to bear witness to that truth: "Jesus Saves."

What exactly is being asked of us? Jesus asks only that we "proclaim" His Good News, not that we should be able to make people believe it. There is no promise that our witnessing to the Gospel will fall on ready ears, or that we should enjoy the least degree of success. Like the Sower in the parable, all we can do is faithfully sow the seeds, then leave the growing to God's grace. In the heart of every evangelist is a determination to give what has been given them. Worship is something we do for God, not for ourselves, and whether or not we enjoy it is a side issue - nice if we do, but still to be done if we don't. In exactly the same way, fruitful Evangelization is God's own work, not ours.

The best witnesses are not the ones who shout loudest or speak most seductively, tricks like that belong to the world of advertising, "spin" and propaganda. No, the best witnesses often have very little to say for themselves.

Saint Francis of Assisi told his follows "Preach the Gospel - and, if absolutely necessary, use words!"

This is a great comfort, because we are often at a loss for the right thing to say. The love of God is something which we can show to people, even if we don't know a word of their language.

"Heart speaks to heart" was the motto of Saint John Henry Newman. Mother (now Saint) Theresa of Calcutta used to tell her followers: "God does not ask us to be successful - just faithful".

Spend time with our endlessly patient and merciful Lord this week. Speak your own words of faith, hesitant though they may sometimes be. Treasure His nearness and love Him in others. Do that, and you'll be the best of witnesses.

Lord, help me so live, that
Those who know me, but not You,
Through me, know You too.

****

4th Sunday of Easter   *Jesus the Good Shepherd.*

Gospel Reading: John 10:11-18

The image of Jesus as the Good Shepherd is both familiar and appealing. Looking through old family photos recently, I lit upon a small snapshot of my late brother James, aged about 9, and flanked by our Great Uncle and Aunt, Jack and Kate Blanchard. They are standing outside the simple cottage in the Lincolnshire Wolds where Jack and Kate lived all of their married life. Uncle Jack was a Shepherd of the "old school". These days very few of us ever see a shepherd with his sheep. The image Jesus used is part of an earlier age, an individual minding a fairly small flock, knowing each one of them, and every sheep knowing, trusting and heeding his voice. I was once privileged to see a Trappist monk with a small flock of sheep belonging to his Abbey. The Trappists are a silent Order, and this applies even when communicating with their animals. He went into the field, clapped his hands, then turned and walked back the way he'd just come. There was no dog, no whistling, no shouting, just that one handclap. The sheep quietly followed him out of the field. Watching that, I came to a new understanding of the Good Shepherd, An image which speaks in silence of the intimacy of that relationship between shepherd and sheep.

There are four important verbs in our short Gospel reading:

BELONG   LISTEN   KNOW   LEAD

The human soul, made by God, hungers for God. We need to know that we belong, but there will be an underlying sense of incompleteness all our lives long. Psalm 27:8 expresses this so well:

"Of you my heart has spoken 'Seek his face'. It is your face, O Lord. that I seek; hide nor your face from me from me."

Philosophers have termed this sense of never quite belonging "alienation". Unfortunately, proposed remedies such as atheistic materialism can only ever make that sense of incompleteness even worse.

The Lord wants to reassure each one of us today that really we do belong, at the same time making it clear that in order to hear His gentle voice, one has "to listen". Are we good at listening to God? Are there spaces and moments in your daily life which you dedicate, in a particular way, to listening to the Word of God? It is necessary to listen in order to hear. It is also necessary to listen if we truly wish to communicate with another person. It is surprising how many people, when asked how they pray, begin by saying: "Well, I just talk to God." Prayer which involves no more than that never gets one very far - it will always remain shallow and dissatisfying. The great

Benedictine spiritual writer Dom Hubert Van Zeller described the sound of a human voice echoing around in the vast emptiness of the self-absorbed soul. Folk who talk incessantly about themselves are very boring - not least to their own selves!

"I know my own, and my own know me." (John 10:14)

Jesus goes on to say that He knows His flock. In the Bible, that word knowing has a much deeper meaning than we would normally understand. For us "knowledge" is often just the possession of bits and pieces of information. In the Bible "knowing" a person is not just knowing about them, but rather an intimate knowledge of a true person in the very depths of their being. Psalm 139, often known as "The Hound of Heaven" opens with the words:

"O Lord, you search me and you know me. You yourself know my resting and my rising; you discern my thoughts from afar."

This is your relationship with Jesus Christ - he knows you better even than you know yourself, and he still loves you - what a friend!

St. Gregory wrote "I assure you that it is not by faith that you will come to know him, but by love; not by mere conviction, but by action" (Homily 14. 3-6)

The next verb is "lead". Where Jesus leads, we must follow. After the Resurrection, Jesus commanded Peter "feed my lambs, feed my sheep", and His parting words to Peter were simply "Follow me" - at their first meeting Jesus had said the exact same. To follow Jesus is no casual commitment or intellectual exercise. No, "following Jesus" involves the whole being of a person: the mind, the heart, the will. Does your consciousness of Christ at a theoretical level find its way into the practicalities of life too, so that you recognise the Good Shepherd's voice, and follow where He leads on life's journey? For someone who has truly listened to His voice, who has knowledge of the reality of His love, that "following" becomes their only path. It is daily, continuous and does not weaken even in the face of future threats, even though we are daily assailed by the clamour of other voices or ideologies which try to snatch us from communion with God.

Our Saviour assures us that, if we listen and follow, and in spite of all of the trials our discipleship will bring, we will never be "lost" or "damned" and nobody will be able to "snatch" us from the presence of Christ who protects our life. This is the foundation and motivation of our daily assurance. This idea is expressed in such a luminous way by Saint Paul:

"For I am certain that neither death nor life, nor angels nor principalities, nor powers, no the present things, nor the future

things, nor strength nor the heights, nor the depths, nor any other created thing, will be able to separate us from the love of God which is in Christ Jesus, our Lord" (Rm 8:38-39).

True following of Jesus is always based on calling and listening. That relationship brings with it the divine assurance of attaining spiritual maturity. The true foundation of this assurance lies in discovering, every day, the divine identity of this Shepherd who is the assurance of our life.

This assurance is not just for today, tomorrow or next week. Jesus says that He gives eternal life, assuring you that the end of your journey as believer is not dark and uncertain. For you, does eternal life refer to the number of years that you can live or instead does it recall your communion of life with God Himself? Is the experience of the company of God in your life a reason for joy?

One last Psalm quotation, from number 100:3 "Know that he, the Lord, is God. He made us, we belong to him; we are his people, the flock of his flock."

Good Shepherd, Jesus,
Loving your flock - every one,
Safe, You'll bring us home.

****

5th Sunday of Easter   *The True Vine*

Gospel reading: John 15:1-8

The image of the vine recurs throughout the Old Testament. In the Book of Exodus, we read that two of the men Moses sent to spy out the Promised Land returned with a cluster of grapes so heavy that it took two men to lift it! Psalm 80:8-9 says to God: "There was a vine: you uprooted it from Egypt, to plant it you drove out other nations" The Prophets use the image again and again: Isaiah proclaims "For the Vineyard of the Lord of hosts is the house of Israel" (5:7). The facade of the Holy Place, the most sacred part of the Jerusalem Temple, was decorated with a solid gold vine, festooned with huge golden grapes.

Sadly, however, the Prophets often had to reprimand their contemporaries for failing to bear good fruit for the Lord (Isaiah 5:1-2, Jeremiah 2:21), and threaten them with destruction by fire (Jeremiah 15:6) - the precious part of the vine is only the fruit, the wood is completely useless, except as firewood, the branches which bore no fruit would be cut off and burned. Psalm 80:12 portrays Israel in exile as a vineyard with broken down walls and wild beasts roaming in it at will.

In His parable of the Tenants of the Vineyard (Mark 12:1-12), Our Lord himself returned to that same familiar theme. The vineyard was still the Lord's property, but the tenants had proved themselves unworthy of it. The meaning of this parable was not lost on Our Lord's enemies.

In our Gospel today, Jesus tells us that He is the True Vine, and that we are the branches. The branches are part of the vine and draw sustenance from it. We belong to Jesus, He is the source of our spiritual nourishment. The branches, however, are not there to be passive "hangers-on" like the parasitic mistletoe which is fed by the oak tree but does nothing in return. We, the branches of the True Vine, have the responsibility of using the nourishment we receive to bear good fruit. This is the Church, a communion of life with Him, fruitful for the benefit of others.

Our Lord goes on to say: "I am the true vine, and my Father is the vinedresser". Just like the rose grower, the vinedresser needs to have a sharp pruning knife which he is not afraid to us. Barren branches must be cut off, so that they do not draw nourishment without purpose. Even the fruitful branches need cutting back so that they will bear even more abundant fruit.

In our Second Reading from Saint John's First Epistle, we heard:

"My little ones, let us not love in words only, but in works and in truth". (1 John 3:18)

Pope Francis teaches us "God wants to bestow new life upon us, full of vitality. Christ came to call sinners. It is they who need the doctor, not the healthy (cf. Lk 5:31f.). Hence, as the Second Vatican Council expresses it, the Church is the "universal sacrament of salvation" (Lumen Gentium, 48), existing for sinners in order to open up to them the path of conversion, healing and life. That is the Church's true and great mission, entrusted to her by Christ." (Visit to Germany 22/9/2011)

Our Lord continues:

"Whoever abides in me, and I in him, he it is who bears much fruit; for apart from me you can do nothing."

and then reminds us of the price we must pay for "doing nothing" -

"If anyone does not abide in me he is thrown like a branch and withers; and the branches are gathered, thrown into the fire, and burned"

Reflecting upon this parable, Saint Augustine says:

"The branch is suitable only for one of two things, either the vine or the fire: if it is not in the vine, its place will be in the fire; and that it may escape the latter, may it have its place in the vine" (In Ioan. Ev. Tract. 81:3 [PL 35, 1842]).

To bear fruit, we must abide in Christ, and so Saint Augustine continues:

"As much as anyone loves the Church of Christ, so much have they the Holy Spirit" (In Ioan. Ev. Tract. 32:8 [PL 35:1646]).

Experience of pruning is seldom pleasant. We can at times misinterpret the graces God gives to make us more fruitful as signs of His disfavour.

It is with, and within the Church that we are able to proclaim to our world the great truth that Christ is alive and is the source of Christian living. He gives himself so that we may have abundant life, and so that we may have a future.

God has no wish for our lives to be barren, lifeless, parasitic or unfruitful. He does not want any of his children to be discarded.

Jesus tells us that He has come so that we might have life, abundant life.
Remain in Jesus,
Bear much fruit; life is barren,
Fruitless, without Him.

****

Feast of the Ascension　　　*Goodbye and Hello*

Gospel reading: Mark 16:15-20

Meditation is a funny thing. We human beings have a great tendency to start thinking about one thing, and then quite suddenly find our minds entirely elsewhere. Some people have the ability to control this better than others. They are the ones with remarkable powers of concentration - the rest of us are the daydreamers. At school, I was certainly one of the latter, as my reports would show, had I not wisely burned them all many years ago! This ability to move effortlessly from one train of thought to another is particularly noticeable in prayer and worship - how often we confess to suffering distractions in prayer. Whilst it is obviously undesirable that we should be thinking about a Lottery win at the moment of the Consecration at Mass, or what colour to paint the front gate during the Rosary, what we term "distraction" is by no means always a bad thing. In the Bible, both Old and New Testaments, we frequently find God communicating through dreams: Jacob (Gen. 28:1-19), Joseph (Gen.37:5), Pharaoh (Gen. 41:1-7), Daniel (Dan. 7) St. Joseph (Mt. 1:20, 2:13, 2:19) St. Peter (Acts 10:10), St. Paul (Acts 16:19) and the Magi (Matt. 2:12) to name but a few instances. St. Peter's description of his moment of great revelation at Jaffa makes it quite clear that this was a dream that took place in the daytime. Sudden thoughts and inspirations coming to mind when we are thinking of other things can be workings of the grace of God and give us unexpected insight into new depths of meaning. The practice of Christian Meditation is one way in which we can harness the wanderings of the mind. In the Eastern traditions of Meditation, the aim is to achieve a wordless, imageless state - in Western Spirituality we would describe that condition as "Contemplative". Contemplation is not something which can be artificially brought about. That entire union of a human mind with the mind of God is sometimes given to people when they are at prayer, but always as a gift. The great Spiritual Teachers of our Church recommend Meditation as a way to progress in prayer. The Scriptures, the teaching of the Church, Religious Art and Music can all provide food for deep and prayerful thought which can lead in unexpected directions. St. Francis de Sales likened this prayer to walking in a beautiful garden where we might pause to admire the colour, shape or aroma of one particular flower. It has been said that a person of deep spirituality is one who Is able to see the whole world in a single flower.

Having heard all of this, you may be wondering what on earth this has to do with the Ascension of Our Lord into Heaven! Let me explain. When I was meditating on today's Gospel, I suddenly found my mind hundreds of miles and centuries away from Mount Olivet in the Holy Land and stood once again on the platform of the railway station in a little village called Haborough, a few miles from my boyhood home in

Lincolnshire. That was a location of many departures and arrivals for our family. It is now almost fifty years since my Dad died, but I will never forget the love he showed in always insisting on being at the station to see me off when I journeyed back to college or parish, and being there to welcome me when I came home. He always said the same thing: "Goodbye boy, and hurry back!", and he would watch the departing train till it was out of sight. I also remember the joy with which every homecoming was greeted. Even when he was no longer well enough to stand on the platform, he would sit waiting in the car park. We didn't kiss and embrace one another, that wasn't his way, but his smile and firm handshake was all it took to show how his heart rejoiced to see me again. He used to say: "If there were no "goodbyes", there would be no "hellos"!"

I stayed my mind on that, and waited to see where God would lead. Gradually the realisation dawned that we tend to regard the Ascension as a "goodbye" and not a "hello". Jesus was passionate in His desire to return to the Father. From His perspective, the Ascension was about going home to His Dad. It was a moment of supreme joy and accomplishment. Our Lord had, as St. Paul tells us "humbled Himself by being obedient to the point of death, even death on a cross" (Philippians 2:8) for us and our salvation Through His Death and Resurrection, Jesus gained new life for all humanity. Job done, He returned to His home in Heaven, to His loving Father. From God's point of view, this was very definitely a "hello" moment.

Truth be told, the Ascension is not really a final "goodbye" moment for any of us. Jesus did not leave us as orphans (cf. John 14:18) - in our Sunday Gospel a few weeks ago we walked with the Disciples on the Emmaus Road, and learned with them that Jesus is truly with us in the Breaking of Bread. The coming of the Holy Spirit at Pentecost has equipped the Church with all the gifts needed to help each individual find Jesus the Way, and through His Truth attain eternal life. For us, the Ascension is one of those "goodbyes" which will surely lead to the joy of another "hello".

The Apostles, we are told, stood around gazing wistfully at the sky after Our Lord's Ascension, but not for long! They were taken to task by the Angel, shaken out of their "brown study", and told to embrace the mission given to them, secure in the knowledge that they would see Jesus again. The saintly Curé of Ars often inspired people in his sermons, not with great learning and oratorical skills, but with the deep sincerity of his repeated "We shall see Him, we shall see Him". This is not a day for feeling abandoned and alone. As Pentecost approaches, it is a for us to rejoice in the Faith God has given us, the Fellowship with which He blesses the Church, and the abiding presence of the Holy Spirit. This is no time for nostalgia, but for looking forward in joyful hope. Between the Our Father and Holy Communion at Mass we always pray for that "Joyful Hope" in the "Coming of our Lord and Saviour Jesus Christ". Our true home is not in this world, but in Heaven. Jesus has promised that He will prepare a place for us, then return and take us with Him (John 14:13) to that place where there are no more "goodbyes".

Surely that is the starting point for many meditations!

****

6th Sunday of Easter   *"Remain in my Love"*

Gospel reading: John 15:9-17

Our Lord speaks to us this morning about relationship with God, with one another, and with the Church.

His teaching always begins with God, within the mystery of the Holy Trinity. "As the Father has loved me, so I have loved you". God is our first beginning and our last end. All creation, the little part we know about, and the vastness of the universe beyond, all began in God. Every single human life both begins and ends in Him.

God is Love. There is a magnificent icon of the Holy Trinity painted by Rublev. It shows the Father, Son and Holy Spirit seated together at a circular table. All three have identical faces, but are differently dressed, the Father in majestic gold, the Son in brown, the earth colour symbolising His incarnation as "A Man like us in all things but sin", and also His Precious Blood, shed for us and for our salvation. The Holy Spirit wears green, the colour of hope and new life. The three figures are looking in love, one at another. This is the best possible image of the Holy Trinity as far as I am concerned. God has one Nature, but exists as three distinct Persons, from all eternity One in love.

There is, however, one more vital element in Rublev's icon. The Three sit at the table, but there remains an empty place, and that represents God's invitation from the moment of our creation for each one of His children to join in that community of love. Out of pure love God created us. Out of pure love He redeemed us through the Death and Resurrection of His Son. We are called into relationship with God. It is our fundamental human vocation, and no human person is complete without it. "You have made us for yourself, and our hearts are restless till we rest in You." (St. Augustine, Confessions)

When Jesus speaks to us of the love which the Father and He have for us and our world, He invites us to grow in an awareness of being in relationship with the Trinity; we are thought of, wanted, gifted, saved between the Father and the Son in the Spirit; presenting our actions in response to the love of God who first called us. That awareness motivates us to love God in return.

But what, after all is "love"? It is certainly a word heard frequently on human lips. One might be forgiven for thinking that it has been rather over-used during our lifetime. As the song says, love means different things to different people. A materialist and entirely subjective interpretation of love can trivialise it to no more than a fleeting emotion, an animal instinct governed by hormones and pheromones. It can be no less trivialised by an over-sentimental spirituality, remember the "Smile, God loves you" stickers, so easily leading to the conclusion that our behaviour had no impact on our relationship with the Creator? Spiritual escapism is not what our Saviour has in mind!

One of the first things a Christian must do is, as Jesus said, is to read the signs of the times - to read reality. Our emotional lives, like the weather, have fine sunny days to be sure, but there are plenty of dark, cloudy and stormy ones as well. True love has to be about more than the way we happen to feel that day; love is a choice we make, a way we decide to behave, and often contrary to our own feelings in the surrounding circumstances. Love is not so much the way I feel as the way I choose to act. So Jesus tells to remain in His love, going on to say that If we keep His commandments, we will remain in His love.

Having recognised the true reality of love, we must then commit to it, giving our life (in all its forms) as a concrete expression and appreciation of love; it is this authentic Christian love which makes us true witnesses to the Gospel in a world that God wishes to save. Last weekend marked the feast of St. Athanasius, the hero of the Council of Nicaea, the source of the Creed we will pray together in a few moments now. He wrote: "The Word made Flesh takes on our human body in all its reality". (Oratio de incarnatione Verbi, 8) In the same way, we must accept our lives in "all their reality", and our relationships too in all their reality, letting both be guided and moulded by the teaching of Jesus. St. John tells us that our love must be not just words or mere talk, but something active and genuine:

"My little children, let us love not only in the words we speak, but truly in our actions" (1 John 3:18, my own translation).

Our human lives are not to be lived in solitary confinement. Homo Sapiens is a social animal. Neither should we even attempt to live our spiritual lives in glorious isolation, that is why we have the Church. The life of the Church is a life of relationship in relationship. Our Church is not only an image of the Trinity but exists "within" the Trinity. There is only one free place at the table of Rublev's Trinity, and that one space is big enough for every single human person, past, present and to come. It is in and through community, especially the community of believers which we call "Church", that we find our place at that table, guided to freedom and joy in the community of believers. The Church is the Mystical Body of Christ on earth. It is not a building, a club, an institution, it is people living in Christ, living by Christ, living with Christ, living as Christ.

This was clearly taught by the Second Vatican Council, and I finish today's little meditation with a few words from the

Pastoral Constitution on the Church in the Modern World, aptly entitled "Gaudium et Spes" - Joy and Hope.

"The Church is the guardian of God's Word, from which are drawn the principles of religious and moral order. Without always having a ready answer to every question, the church desires to integrate the light of revelation with the skills and knowledge of mankind, so that it may shine on the path which humanity has lately entered."

"Man, created in God's image has been commissioned to master the Earth and all it contains, and so to rule the world in justice and holiness. He is to acknowledge God as the creator of all, and to see himself and the whole universe in relation to God, in order that all things may be subject to man, and God's name be an object of wonder and praise over all the Earth. This commission extends to even the most ordinary activities of everyday life. Where men and women, in the course of gaining livelihood for themselves and their families, offer appropriate service to society, they can be confident that their personal efforts promote the work of the Creator, confirm benefit on the fellow man, and help to realise God's plan in history." (#33,34)

Jesus calls us friends,

He tells us "Keep my commands,

Remain in my love."

****

7th Sunday of Easter *Consecrate them in the truth.*

The Gospel reading today was an extract from Our Lord's Priestly Prayer at the Last Supper. We heard Him ask His Father to keep those He had given to His Son true to His name, so that they we may become one just as He and the Father are one. He also prays that we may be consecrated in the truth. In this prayer, Jesus returns to two themes we have already identified in earlier Eastertide Gospels: the first is the invitation of the Holy Trinity, Father, Son, and Spirit for each one of us to become united with God in faith and love. This calls for a recognition of the fact that we human beings, created by God, are incomplete without Him. The second theme is our need to be people whose lives are grounded in reality, able to tell the difference between truth and falsehood.

A few days ago, we celebrated the Feast of Saint Matthias, the new Apostle chosen to fill the place within the Twelve caused by the death of Judas Iscariot, who had betrayed Jesus. Saint Peter's description of the ideal candidate is revealing: "One of the men who have accompanied us all the time that the Lord Jesus went in and out among us" (Acts 1:21). Devoted supporters of philosophies and political systems are often called "Fellow Travellers" - the Native Americans have a proverb "To know a man, you must walk in his moccasins" - this was surely what Peter had in mind. The single most essential quality in any Christian is that they have spent much time with Jesus. No amount of reading, courses or lectures in spirituality can bring one to a personal encounter with Jesus - this comes only through personal commitment to Him in private prayer and scripture reading, and it is no easy matter either. It is this personal friendship which both makes us see what should be done and gives us the strength to do it. We read in Psalm 119 "Your word is a lamp for my feet, a light on my path" (v.105). Chapter 8 of the Second Book of "The Imitation of Christ" is entitled "Of Friendship with Jesus", and tells us: "When Jesus is present, all goes well, and nothing seems difficult, but when Jesus is absent, everything is hard. When Jesus does not speak within us, nothing can give us comfort, but if Jesus speaks just one word, we feel great consolation."

Saint Peter went on to say that what was expected of the apostle was that he could act with his fellow Apostles as a witness to Christ's Resurrection. That word "witness" is of great importance. Pope Saint Paul VI, speaking of the proclamation of the Gospel in our own time, wrote: "Modern man listens more willingly to witnesses than to teachers, and if he does listen to teachers, it is because they are witnesses." (Evangelii Nuntiandi (1975) no. 41). Recently, we celebrated the Feast of the Ascension, when the Gospel reading told of Our Lord's parting instructions to the Church: "Go into all world and proclaim the gospel to the whole creation" (Mark 16:18) What exactly is being asked of us? Jesus asks only that we "proclaim" His Good News, not that we should be able to make people believe it. There is no promise that our witnessing to the Gospel will fall on ready ears, or that we should enjoy the least degree of success. Like the Sower in the parable, all we can do is faithfully sow the seeds, then leave the growing to God's grace. True Liturgy is something we do for God, not for ourselves. In exactly the same way, fruitful Evangelization is God's own work, not ours. As I earlier remarked, Mother (now Saint) Theresa of Calcutta used to tell her followers: "God does not ask us to be successful - but only to be faithful".

I used to enjoy hill walking. It is quite easy to get lost in Snowdonia, the Lake District or the High Peak, unwary walkers do it all the time. Good ramblers learn the importance of having clear reference points, and knowing how to read a map and compass when visibility is poor. Today's Gospel gives us such very clear reference-points for our spiritual journey.

We need God if we are to be complete as human beings. Faith is not a "feeling", it is a choice. Faith means entering into a relationship with the Blessed Trinity, Father, Son and Holy Spirit through making time, real quality time for God, day by day. God knows you and me better than we know our own selves, so our journey of faith will reveal to us unwelcome aspects of our own selves, and temptation is never far away either. In the Old Testament story of Cain and Abel, God warns the angry, jealous Cain: "Sin is crouching at the door" (Genesis 4:7). This is all part of the reality in which we need to be grounded. It is the surest defence against perhaps the greatest of all temptations - pride. Be grateful when you are made to "feel small", because in truth we all are!

Jesus asked the Father: "Sanctify them in the truth, your word is truth" (John 17:17). We need to recognise the falsehood of living as though we "belonged to the world". None of us is resident here for very long. The temptation to materialism, to the pursuit of success, wealth and celebrity will "crouch at our door" as long as we live. We need also to see that the worst lies we ever tell are the ones we tell ourselves, the prejudices, false judgements and self-justification to which we can fall prey.

As Eastertide draws to its close, can we pray especially that God's word will be a Lamp for our feet, a light for our eyes, and that knowing the truth about God, and about our own selves, will make us faithful witnesses too.

****

Pentecost Sunday   *Not as Orphans*

Gospel reading: John 20:19-23

"Alleluia! Not as orphans are we left in sorrow now." Reassuring words from a much-loved hymn, (Alleluia! Sing to Jesus, William C. Dix 1867) Last week, we heard the consoling words Jesus spoke to His first followers: "I will not leave you as orphans" (John 14:18). Jesus promised the gift of the Holy Spirit. Today we celebrate the fulfilment of that promise. God's Church has been gifted with the Holy Spirit, as a whole and in each and every individual member. On the first Pentecost Sunday, the Apostles experienced the coming of the Holy Spirit in an awesome, powerful, life-changing and dramatic way. It is possible for us to become so blinded by the "epic" of the Church's birth that we lose sight of a great truth: "This promise is for you." (Acts 2:39). Yes, the Gift of that same Holy Spirit is given to each and every one of us, and today I would like to share with you just two thoughts about receiving that gift.

Over my years as a priest, I have heard many people speak of their experience of Confirmation, often with confusion and a sense of disappointment afterwards. One might summarise their words as follows: "We heard the story of Pentecost and of great Saints who had done marvellous things in the power of the Holy Spirit. We were told that we would receive the same Spirit. We were prepared for something great and exciting to happen, but after receiving the Sacrament we felt no different."

I think that there is a common mistake in catechesis which is somewhat akin to a school teacher who so desires to give her pupils a love for great literature that she forgets to teach them to read first! Pope Francis has spoken of what he calls "Spiritual Illiteracy". (Homily for Pentecost 2016)

This is certainly manifest when people can only believe in spiritual experience on an emotional level. In Spiritual Direction and Pastoral Counselling, I have often found that a lack of feeling in prayer and worship can lead the unwary to conclude that they are spiritually dead and failing Christians. It can be such a relief for them to learn for the first time the basic spiritual truth that the faculties of the soul are Memory, Understanding and Will. Emotion is nowhere in it! The most cursory reading of the lives of the Saints reveals that the best and holiest of people experienced years of spiritual dryness, finding no delight or consolation in prayer at all. What makes them saints is the fact that they persevered in their efforts to love and serve God and Neighbour, even when it seemed to bring nothing at all to their own selves. Saint Ignatius prayed that he might "Fight and not heed the wounds, labour and seek for no reward save that of knowing that in all things I am doing Thy most holy will." His Spiritual Exercises are matter-of-fact and often austere in their practicality, yet they have brought millions closer to God, and continue to do so today. The New Testament is clear that the immediate need of the Apostles on the first Pentecost Sunday was for <u>COURAGE</u>. That same gift is available to every confirmed person. People who have done extraordinarily brave deeds invariably tell of the personal terror which possessed them at an emotional level, but was overcome with an act of will. This again is clearly descriptive of the Holy Spirit at work.

"Not as orphans are we left". My second thought today is about the importance of family for all of us. There is a cynical and oft-repeated aphorism "God gave me my family, but in His mercy permitted me to choose my friends!", and maybe there are times when we might feel inclined to agree. That said, however, few really believe that to be true. One only need witness the loneliness and vulnerability of the orphaned child or the desolation of the neglected old person to see how very important family is. We constantly come across stories of people going to extraordinary lengths to trace children given up for adoption at birth, or the adopted ones seeking their birth parents. Not all of these stories have a happy ending: sometimes the adoptive parents feel rejected, and sometimes the birth parents have no wish to be found. Nevertheless, the instinct to seek family, the need to belong, is a compelling motive.

The Holy Spirit, Saint Paul tells us, makes us the adopted

sons and daughters of our Father in Heaven, confident to call Him "Abba" (Daddy). We are Sons and Daughters "in the Son" (cf. Romans 8:14-17), with Jesus as our older Brother. Our Lord gave us Mary to be our Mother (cf. John 19:26). If we are all children of the same Heavenly Father, it follows that we are all brothers and sisters one with another.

Getting back to the way we feel about things, it may well be that our experience of home and family is not always one we feel all that good about, maybe our relatives are demanding, tedious and unappreciative at times, but it would be a very poor parent who used the bad behaviour of a child as an excuse for neglecting their own responsibilities. In the same way, the crankiness of an elderly parent would be no justification for their children to "wash their hands" of them.

Our adoption as sons and daughters of the one Father, and as brothers and sisters in Christ, brings its own responsibilities. Even though that great family may not always be a lot of fun, they are still family, and we are not free simply to walk away.

Perhaps the correct question for every confirmed person to ask on Pentecost Sunday is not "How should Confirmation make me feel?" But "How should I, as a child of God, be living my life?" In the 25th Chapter of Saint Matthew's Gospel we are given a clear picture of the Day of Judgement. The "Blessed of my Father" whom Christ the Judge calls into the Kingdom of Heaven looked after their brothers and sisters, but they didn't feel particularly virtuous in so doing. The damned didn't feel bad about their neglect of those in need. They were not judged on how they had felt, only about the way they acted.

"But with regard to the breath of God, it not only warms, but also gives perfect light, His Spirit being an infinite Spirit, whose vital breath is called inspiration, because by it the Divine Goodness breathes upon us, and inspires us with the desires and intentions of His heart." (St. Frances de Sales Treatise on Love of God VIII. 7, Tr. H. Macken, Burns & Oates 1884)

May the Holy Spirit give us all the wisdom and understanding to know ourselves as children of God, and the courage to live accordingly.

****

Ref:040923/ 31619 143 VM4-12

Printed in Great Britain
by Amazon

28543584R00079